Barbie

Contents

Parts of this edition were previously published.

Margot Robbie wore dozens of outfits in Barbie, including this glittery jumpsuit.

From Cultural Icon to Box Office Champ

BARBIE'S BEEN A HOUSEHOLD NAME FOR
MORE THAN 60 YEARS, BUT IT TOOK CAREFUL,
CAUTIOUS PLANNING BEFORE MATTEL
WAS READY TO MAKE HER A MOVIE STAR.

BY ELIANA DOCKTERMAN

BARBIE IS AN ICON, PERHAPS THE BEST KNOWN toy in the world. As Margot Robbie pointed out in an interview for a TIME cover story, the word "Barbie" has the sort of enviable global recognition only achieved by brands like Coca-Cola. Since her debut in 1959, Barbie has been a staple of the culture, a touchpoint for pop icons like Nicki Minaj, and has become synonymous with a specific shade of pink.

And yet it somehow took until 2023 for Barbie to make her live-action film debut. While there have been a number of animated Barbie movies and series on Nickelodeon and streaming services, *Barbie* is the first live-action film starring the doll to premiere in theaters. Robbie plays a version of Bar-

bie, but so do Issa Rae, Kate McKinnon, Hari Nef, Alexandra Shipp, and a number of other actors. Ryan Gosling plays just one of many Kens. Every image from the film, beginning with the first paparazzi shots of Robbie and Gosling roller-blading in spandex, has been dissected online, and the "Barbiecore" fashion trend has never been hotter.

The journey to get here was complicated. Over the years, other potential Barbie movies have come and gone. The toy company and filmmakers struggled with how to deal with Barbie's baggage: The traditionally thin-waisted, blonde-haired doll has long been criticized for setting unrealistic body standards. Even after Mattel introduced a "curvy"

Barbie rode waves of nostalgia and curiosity to quickly become the year's buzziest film.

Barbie in 2016, the original Barbie has stuck in people's minds.

Plus, Barbie is intentionally a blank slate upon which girls can project their dreams and desires. That made conjuring one specific story for the movie particularly difficult. "As simple as an 11-and-a-half-inch doll looks, Barbie is a complicated brand," says Richard Dickson, the president and COO of Mattel until July 2023, when he left the company to be CEO of Gap Inc.

But when Mattel CEO Ynon Kreiz took over the company in 2018, he decided it was time to commit to a Barbie movie. The film would be the first entry in a burgeoning cinematic universe based on the company's toys. That same year, Robbie signed on to produce and star in *Barbie*, and a year later, Warner Bros. announced that Greta Gerwig and Noah Baumbach had joined as screenwriters.

Why did it take so long? Mattel has been incredibly cautious when it comes to its most valuable asset—and rightly so. Barbie has spent much of her history as the best-selling doll in the world. Devotees would tell you that she inspires little girls to imagine themselves in any profession—astronaut, president, veterinarian. But the doll and her creators have also been called out by parents concerned about how she affects their children's self-esteem. Over the years, songs like Aqua's "Barbie Girl" and even throwaway lines in movies like *Legally Blonde*—when a Harvard Law student disdainfully calls Elle Woods "Malibu Barbie"—have not exactly bolstered Barbie's reputation as a figure of female empowerment.

Any portrayal of Barbie on screen would be inherently fraught, and the company hasn't always had a sense of humor about the doll. When Barbie appeared as a supporting character in *Toy Story 3* and *Toy Story 4* in the 2010s, Mattel creatives emphasized to me that it was a big deal that the company ceded any control to Pixar and allowed the studio to poke fun at Barbie and Ken. Years earlier, Mattel had sued the Europop band Aqua over "Bar-

> Barbie is intentionally a blank slate upon which girls can project their dreams and desires. That made conjuring one specific story for the movie particularly difficult.

bie Girl." Cut to 2023, and one of the most popular songs on the *Barbie* soundtrack is Nicki Minaj and Ice Spice's "Barbie World," which samples Aqua.

When Amy Schumer signed on to play the doll in a live-action movie in 2016, the comedian had cemented herself as a sharp feminist voice in pop culture. Her Comedy Central sketch show, *Inside Amy Schumer*, had no mercy when it came to skewering the patriarchy. It was difficult to imagine that Mattel, a company that had spent millions maintaining an immaculate image for its doll, would submit to Schumer's particular brand of humor. Indeed, Schumer recently said she left the movie because that version wasn't "feminist and cool."

Dickson, who had been with the company long enough to see several potential films come and go, argues that until Gerwig, the company "never found the right storyteller" for Barbie. Mattel is now eager to prove it is in on the joke. In Gerwig's film, the company is run by executives who take umbrage at anyone who points out that it's strange so many men in suits are running a brand for little girls. And the movie acknowledges Barbie's complicated impact on girls' body image.

Rae, who plays President Barbie, points out that calling someone a Barbie "does have a negative connotation. You're like, 'Oh that person might be a bimbo. That person might be dumb. That person is superficial.' This movie presents an opportunity not to change that, but add more onto it and clear her name in a pretty cool way."

Gerwig also seems to have a love for the doll that transcends that of the typical filmmaker. "One of the most endearing parts of the process with Greta was her appreciation of the brand's history," says Dickson. "It was a matter of finding the right talent that can appreciate the brand's authenticity and bring that controversy to life in a way that, yes, pokes fun at us but ultimately is purposeful and has heart."

But even signing on to Gerwig's version took some effort on the part of Mattel. Robbie Brenner, the first executive producer of Mattel Films, told

executives they would have to "white-knuckle it" through the creative process with Gerwig and Baumbach and learn that a dose of self-deprecation can go a long way.

Of course, the question of who, exactly, would play Barbie was paramount. Mattel recently took great pains to modernize the doll. Nearly a decade ago, in 2014, Barbie had a very bad year: The Elsa doll from *Frozen* dethroned her as the most popular toy for girls, and Lego surpassed Mattel as the biggest toy company. Sinking sales forced Mattel to rethink the brand, which manifested in the introduction of new skin tones and hair types in 2015 and new body shapes in 2016.

Another reason Mattel resisted putting Barbie on the big screen for so long was that the company had worked to establish that Barbie wasn't just a skinny beach-bound blonde. There are, in fact, 175 different Barbies with different hair, skin tones,

Above: Barbie meets the head of Mattel, played by Will Farrell; opposite, the company's executives, CEO Ynon Kreiz (left) and former COO Richard Dickson (right).

body shapes, and abilities. If Amy Schumer or Anne Hathaway (who was also once attached to play the doll) stood in for Barbie, an otherwise blank canvas would forever be connected to a single actor. If it worked, profits would grow. If it didn't, decades of Mattel's efforts would be undone.

A Barbie movie probably never would have come to fruition if it weren't for Mattel CEO Kreiz. He took over the position at a moment of vulnerability for the company. He was the fourth CEO in just four years. He articulated a vision for Mattel that was rooted in intellectual property management. That plan in-

nomination, for *I, Tonya*—who he thought would be a perfect ambassador for the brand.

It turned out that Robbie was as eager to meet with Mattel as the company was to court her. She thought Barbie would make sense for her production company, LuckyChap Entertainment. "We were kind of keeping tabs on the property for a while before there was an opening, and then we could jump in and say, 'We'd like to produce this. Here's how we would do it and who we would want to do it with,'" she says, "i.e., someone like Greta—Greta being the top of the list, pie in the sky, dream person."

And then there was the creation of this *Barbie,* a process that wound up taking five years. The biggest challenge was dreaming up the right story. "She doesn't have a set narrative. I've played characters where there's source material, comic books, or if it's a real person, archival footage," says Robbie. "Even with fictional characters, there's a story you end up rooting it in." Barbie, by contrast, has no personality by design. The idea is for little kids to project jobs and stories onto her. So Gerwig and Baumbach had to build not just a character, but a story, and an entire world, from scratch.

"Before Greta, we did hear many pitches," says Brenner. "I don't want to call them generic, because that wouldn't be fair. They were all interesting in their own right. But it was sort of predictable. You're thinking, 'That's not enough. We needed to live up to the legacy and the complexity.'"

What Gerwig has conjured is certainly complex. She has fulfilled the presumed corporate mandate: Make a fun summer romp. The film is stuffed with its director's idiosyncrasies, from dance numbers inspired by Old Hollywood to her personal preoccupation with stories about complicated mother-daughter relationships. It obviously connected with the public, as fans flocked to movie theaters, setting box office records and dominating the summer conversation. Kreiz hopes the movie will put Mattel Films on the map: "We're looking to create movies that become cultural events." ❤

cluded more streaming shows, games, a theme park, and movies. Lots of movies. An entire universe of movies. "Once you think of all those people who buy your product not just as consumers but as fans, you realize you have an audience, and all these other opportunities become obvious," Kreiz says.

Marvel and DC have found tremendous success making dozens of films based on stories that already had a built-in fan base of comics readers. But it just so happens that film audiences seem to be tiring of superheroes. Studios are now in search of other known intellectual properties that have not yet been adapted into film. Audiences are ready for something new, if still a bit familiar.

Kreiz believed Mattel was sitting on a gold mine of well-known brands—Barbie, Hot Wheels, American Girl, even the Magic 8 Ball. So he created Mattel Films, a studio inside the company, and hired Oscar-nominated producer Brenner (*Dallas Buyers Club*) to run the show. Mattel has since announced 15 movies, including a Rock 'Em Sock 'Em Robots film with Vin Diesel.

But Kreiz determined that Mattel's first cinematic outing should focus on the company's crown jewel: Barbie. Just four weeks into his tenure as CEO, he requested a meeting with Margot Robbie—who had recently earned her first Academy Award

America's Sweetheart

BARBIE'S ARRIVAL TRANSFORMED THE
TOY BUSINESS, TURNED MATTEL INTO A
FINANCIAL POWERHOUSE, AND CHANGED
THE WAY WE THINK ABOUT DOLLS.

Birth of a Superstar

THANKS TO THE RISKY PLAN OF A DETERMINED
BUSINESSWOMAN, BARBIE ARRIVED IN 1959
AND REVOLUTIONIZED THE TOY INDUSTRY—
AND THE CULTURE AT LARGE.

BY ELIANA DOCKTERMAN

ITH HER WASP WAIST and full bosom, long legs and demure gaze, there was nothing baby-like about this doll. Her lips were red, her brows arched. One of her dresses, snug-bodiced and full-skirted, evoked Christian Dior. She was 11.5 inches of pure grown-up. The time was March 1959, and Mattel's "teenage fashion model" was making her national debut in a television commercial. As the camera pulled back to reveal the toy full-length, she was introduced by a lilting vocalist who cooed her name and her praises: "Barbie, you're beautiful."

And beautiful she was, right down to her pedicured toes. Barbie was also, Mattel knew, completely different from the dozens of dolls crowding toy-store shelves across America. Mattel was betting that she was exactly the alternative young girls wanted. The toymaker was right. Although Barbie sales were slow at the start, in early summer there was a sudden spike, and orders began pouring in to company headquarters in Hawthorne, California. By the end of the year, 300,000 Barbies had been sold. Mattel would not catch up with demand for three more years.

"For boomers, it was one of those watershed moments, like Elvis returning from the army or the arrival of the Beatles in 1964," observed M.G. Lord in her 1994 book, *Forever Barbie: The Unauthorized Biography of a Real Doll*. "She was sunshine, Tomorrowland, and the future made plastic."

From the beginning, Barbie (full name: Barbara Millicent Roberts) defied conventions and expectations. In 1959, only about a third of adult women in the United States worked, yet Barbie owed her existence to Ruth Handler, Mattel's hard-charging, 43-year-old co-owner and executive vice president.

Barbie was brought to market despite the skepticism of male executives at the company, who insisted the doll would be too difficult to produce, and resistance from retailers, who deemed her mature shape inappropriate for young customers. Barbie was one of the first toys whose public persona was buffed by motivational research and focus groups. She was also marketed directly to children through television commercials instead of to the parents who bought the dolls, a strategy pioneered by Mattel that revolutionized the industry. More important, Barbie tapped into a market that other toymakers hadn't realized existed: 5- to 12-year-old girls who dreamed of adulthood, not just as mothers and homemakers but as independent young women who could be whomever they wanted.

Barbie's runaway success transformed her. Between her introduction in 1959 and 1965, she pushed Mattel's sales up sevenfold. She was no longer just an object but an animated symbol—of the changing times, of the booming economy, of the country's values. With one foot in Cold War conservatism and the other in the coming sexual revolution, Barbie represented the evolving American woman. Her wardrobe, too, captured the new range of roles. She could reflect Eisenhower-era wholesomeness (the Friday Night Date set, a blue corduroy jumper and white blouse, came with two glasses and straws) and jet-set chic (Winter Holiday included ski pants, a white vinyl car coat, and an overnight case). She could be a professional in business garb (Busy Gal) or, in her strapless sequined cocktail gown, a sultry torch singer (Solo in the Spotlight).

Barbie was not the only non–baby doll of the time, or even the nation's first fashion doll. The 1950s gave rise to Lingerie Lou as well as Miss Revlon, a bid to create loyal future buyers of lipstick and face powder. Some did pretty well. In 1953, sales of the Vogue "Ginny" dolls, whose wardrobe included

In a 2019 exhibition at the French toy museum *La Nef des Jouets*, the original Barbie stood alongside a Handler family photograph.

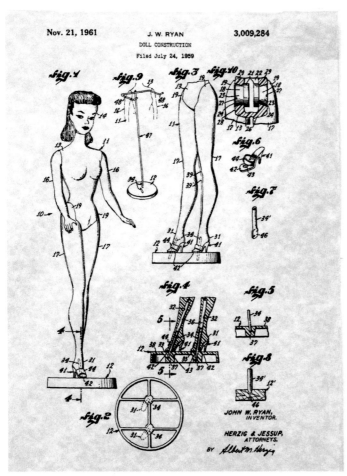

The patent for the original Barbie and a German ad for Bild Lilli, the doll that inspired her.

tweedy business suits and sundresses with matching bloomers, stood at $2.1 million. By 1957, it had climbed to $5 million. But most of these dolls had pudgy faces and rounded bellies. They were a hybrid, not womanly or even girlish. They were toddlers in women's clothing and "encouraged mothering as play," wrote Linda Scott in *Fresh Lipstick*, a 2005 book about fashion and feminism. Playing Barbie, instead, was a "grand adventure."

THE GOLDEN AGE OF THE TOY INDUSTRY in the United States dates to the turn of the 20th century, a period that saw the introduction of talking dolls, the Erector Set, the Flexible Flyer sled, Crayola crayons, and Lincoln Logs. Though inexpensive German-made imports still dominated the U.S. market, the outbreak of World War I in 1914 changed the dynamic as the flow of European toys came to a halt. To fill the void, U.S. makers cranked out dozens of low-priced offerings. By the time the war was over in 1918, there were more than 600 domestic toy manufacturers.

The toy business ticked down during World War II due to labor and material shortages, yet by the time Mattel Inc. was born in 1945, the business was reinventing itself, thanks to the introduction of plastic. Mattel, in fact, originally made plastic picture frames and dollhouse furniture, founded by Elliot Handler and Harold "Matt" Matson ("Mattel" was a mash-up of Matt and Elliot). When, a couple of years later, start-up pressures got to be too much for Matson, he sold his share to his partner, and Ruth Handler joined her husband as the company's official co-owner.

The Handlers had their first hit with the Uke-A-Doodle, a plastic ukelele. Business took off from there. There was a music-box mechanism that went into more than 60 million toys, from guitars to lullaby cribs. Another success was a miniature record-player device that allowed Chatty Cathy to speak. By 1952, Mattel was logging more than $5 million in sales and had completed a 60,000-square-foot factory in Los Angeles.

The biggest toymaker of the era was Louis Marx and Company, a New York–based firm that made its fortune with windup tinplate toys, yo-yos, toy cars, train sets, and play sets depicting scenes such as battlefields and dinosaur-filled landscapes. The company was run by the colorful Louis Marx, who carried toys and neckties in his pockets to give away, the ties embroidered with the Latin phrase *Dum Vivimus, Vivamus*—roughly, "Live it up." Marx started in the business finding ways to undercut established toymakers and earned a reputation as the Henry Ford of the toy industry. In the mid-1950s, he was producing more than 5,000 different toys annually.

The Handlers' goal was to overtake the likes of Marx, and with their next hit, the Burp Gun—plus an assist from the Walt Disney Company—they appeared to be on their way. The Burp Gun was a replica of a paratrooper's machine gun that could fire 50 shots with one pull of the trigger. As Mattel made marketing plans for the toy weapon to coincide with the 1955 Toy Fair in New York City, the Handlers were approached by Disney to sponsor a new program aimed at children, *The Mickey Mouse Club*.

Advertising on television was not new for toymakers; they often ran promotions before Christmas, when the industry raked in 80 percent of its sales, or as part of 13- or 26-week sponsorship deals. But because ABC, which would carry the program, projected that 75 percent of homes with televisions would see *The Mickey Mouse Club*, the deal was contingent on a sponsor making a yearlong commitment. The Handlers agreed, earmarking $500,000, the company's entire net worth, for the ad campaign. When *The Mickey Mouse Club* debuted in

late fall, it was a huge success, and by Christmas, the Handlers had shipped 1 million Burp Guns—including one to the White House, after President Eisenhower wrote to request one for his grandson, David.

Thousands of miles east, a different kind of plaything was released: a doll, Bild Lilli, named for a comic strip that ran in German tabloid *Bild-Zeitung*. The cartoon character Lilli was a curvy, scantily clad gold digger, and the comic followed her exploits. In one strip, Lilli was warned by a police officer that it was illegal to wear her two-piece bathing suit on the boardwalk. "Oh, and in your opinion, which part should I take off?" she asked. Lilli was so popular, in 1955, the toymaker Greiner & Hausser introduced a doll version as a gag gift for men. She was made of hard plastic, with a blonde ponytail and, as M.G. Lord describes them, "Nefertiti eyes."

Barbara Handler, Ruth and Elliot's daughter, turned 14 that year and was too old for dolls. But when Barbara was younger, she and her friends had rejected Betsy Wetsy, Raggedy Ann, and others that encouraged maternal role play. Instead, they spent hours with grown-up-looking paper dolls that came with elaborate wardrobes the girls would cut out and use for their games of make-believe, projecting their future selves onto the small figures. For years, Ruth had tried to convince designers at Mattel to create a three-dimensional version of Barbara's favorites. She got nowhere. The designers, all men, had objected, saying that such a mature-looking doll would not sell because mothers would not buy it for their daughters. What's more, creating such a doll, one who looked like a teenager or college student or career woman, would be too difficult and expensive, and making the tiny clothes that Ruth described, with pleats and bias-cut fabrics, would be impossible.

Yet the effort had not proved too challenging for Greiner & Hausser, and in 1956, while on vacation in Europe, Ruth found the doll she had been describing to her staff: Bild Lilli. In oft-repeated toy-industry lore, Handler and her two children,

> Mattel's designers, all men, had objected to Ruth Handler's idea, saying that such a mature-looking doll would not sell because mothers would not buy it for their daughters.

Barbie's German precursor, Bild Lilli (opposite, flirting with a puppet), was introduced in the 1950s. Above: Decades before the term cosplay originated, a German woman dressed as Lilli in 1954.

Barbara and Ken, were wandering the streets of Lucerne, Switzerland, one day when they came across a toy shop with a window display featuring a very adult-looking doll that had become popular with young girls. While Ken bolted inside, Ruth and Barbara stood outside to admire Lilli. Like her successor, Lilli was 11.5 inches tall and had a small waist, large breasts, and long legs. She was wearing a fashion-forward outfit. Ruth bought two of the dolls, and later, when she came across more versions, purchased those as well.

Upon Ruth's return to California, Mattel's staff got their marching orders: Create an adult fashion doll. If it wasn't possible in the United States, they should look elsewhere. When the company's top designer, Jack Ryan, set off for Tokyo on a business trip, Ruth handed him a Lilli and told him to find a manufacturing partner. There were a couple of stumbling blocks. The Japanese at first were put

off by the doll's looks, according to *Forever Barbie*, because "she looked kind of mean." Plus, Mattel wanted their doll to be a soft vinyl that required her to be rotation-molded, a specialized technology. But the company persisted and within a few months signed a deal with a novelty maker.

As production plans moved ahead for the doll— by this time dubbed Barbie, after the Handlers' daughter—Ruth looked to developing its wardrobe. The choice was less about a love of fashion than a strategy for a healthy revenue stream. Elliot referred to it as "the razor and razor blade" model: You get consumers hooked on the razor (or doll, in this case) and they have to buy the blades (dresses), he told TIME in 1962. Through an art school in Los Angeles, the Handlers found a design instructor, Charlotte Johnson, to take charge of outfitting Barbie. Meticulous and sophisticated, Johnson was the perfect fit for Mattel. She had worked briefly on

zippers, seamstresses who could sew tiny darts and hems, and accessories such as bags and hats. "We are not designing doll clothes, as such, but miniature fashions executed to scale," Johnson said in 1964. "Everything is very intricate, and everything has to be extremely accurate."

IF EVER THERE WERE A time to introduce a product that appealed to the aspirational American, it was the late 1950s. In the postwar boom years, the country had embraced consumer culture with gusto; buying was viewed as a patriotic act. Rising in tandem with consumerism was Madison Avenue. In the 1950s, advertising spending nearly doubled, from $5.7 billion in 1950 to $11.3 billion in 1959, a greater percentage increase than seen in the gross national product or any other economic index, according to the Kenneth E. Behring Center at the Smithsonian's National Museum of American History.

One of the most influential figures in the ad industry was Ernest Dichter, a marketer and psychologist who had pioneered the field of motivational research. Among Dichter's early clients were *Esquire* magazine and Chrysler, both of which he advised—with a nod to his compatriot Sigmund Freud—to employ sexual suggestion to reach consumers. *Esquire* editors, for example, were told that scantily clad women would sell magazines. Chrysler, in contrast, was advised that sedans were like wives, "comfortable and safe," but convertibles were like mistresses, "youthful and beckoning," Robin Gerber reported in her 2009 book, *Barbie and Ruth*.

Seventh Avenue, New York City's fashion district, and was divorced and self-supporting—a career woman, like Ruth. She was also opinionated and demanding and, from the beginning, a key force in shaping and creating Barbie.

At first, Johnson and Ruth met and brainstormed after hours in the Handlers' apartment. The women worked through Barbie's closet with deliberation. They wanted clothes not just for parties and prom but also picnics and travel, for hanging out with friends and for going to the office. Eventually Johnson left the art school and joined Mattel full time, though she often found herself in Japan working with suppliers to find fabrics of the right weight and quality. She needed teeny buttons and snaps and

To Ruth, Dichter was singularly qualified to devise a marketing plan for Barbie and other Mattel toys. He began with in-depth interviews of 191 girls and 45 mothers to determine Barbie's ideal personality. Should she be a good girl, beloved, or self-centered and vain? Would girls play with her?

Barbie has always been a fashion trendsetter with a wide variety of outfits fitting the era (including the 1960s, here and opposite).

The Barbie business engine is fueled not just by the dolls but the endless stream of accessories, including apparel, jewelry, play sets, vehicles, pets, and more.

Would their mothers let them? The deeper he got into his research, the more Dichter realized the challenge: Girls loved Barbie, but their mothers did not. "I know little girls want dolls with high heels, but I object to that sexy costume," one mother remarked while pointing to a pink negligee. "I wouldn't walk around the house in an outfit like that. I don't like that influence on my little girl."

What Mattel needed to do, Dichter concluded, was win over parents. Mothers wanted their daughters to be well groomed; Barbie had beautiful clothes. The trick was to convince Mom that Barbie would make a "poised little lady out of her raffish, unkempt, possibly boyish child," Lord wrote in *Forever Barbie*. "Remind Mom what she believes deep down but dares not express: Better her daughter should appeal in a sleazy way to a man than be unable to attract one at all." To that end, Dichter recommended the Handlers package each outfit with a catalog of other clothes and show Barbie engaged in teenage activities in commercials.

With their marketing strategy set, all that was left for the Handlers was to convince buyers at the March 1959 International American Toy Fair in New York, a raucous affair of buyers, sellers, spies, and hawkers in costume passing out gifts. Ruth dressed Barbie to make a splash. In her strapless black-and-white bathing suit, gold hoop earrings, stiletto heels, and cat-eye sunglasses, she looked like no other doll. Yet there was little enthusiasm among buyers. The representative for Sears rejected Barbie as too sexual. Other buyers followed suit, and while some made commitments, they were mostly small.

Returning to California crestfallen, Ruth began canceling orders. Barbie was a flop.

Until she wasn't. Suddenly, when school was out, kids began clamoring for the doll. Ruth couldn't meet demand. Buyers who had snubbed her at the Toy Fair were now begging for shipments. Barbie was a hit—and she would continue to be for decades.

I N 1959, THE YEAR OF BARBIE'S MARKET debut, she sold more than 300,000 units, and over the next three years she helped balloon Mattel sales from $25 million in 1960 to $75 million in 1962. In 1965, she also helped push the company past the $100 million mark and into the ranks of the Fortune 500. The 1992 release of Totally Hair Barbie—the best-selling Barbie of all time, with some 10 million dolls sold—helped propel Barbie's performance at the checkout counter from $430 million in 1987 to $1 billion by the end of 1992. "Double Sales," marveled the *New York Times* in a headline. "With That Hair, Barbie's Looking Like a Billion."

Today, Barbie is sold in more than 150 countries and represents a fifth of Mattel's business. Sales of Barbie products in 2022 reached nearly $1.5 billion. By the time the *Barbie* movie opened to a record-setting box office total in July 2023, there were more than 3 million followers on the @Barbie Instagram account. Most toys last on the market for two to three years. Barbie's reign has endured for more than six decades.

If anything accounts for the doll's longevity, it is Mattel's careful stewardship of the brand. No target has been too big or too small for the company to go after: Mattel has sued a long list of toy-industry competitors, a fine-art photographer, songwriters, a Canadian restaurant group, and even a Hindi filmmaker for trademark or copyright infringement. It has created copycats of dolls that threatened to eat into or even nibble at Barbie profits, and it has spent lavishly to insulate Barbie from threats. At the same time, Barbie has reaped the benefits of her own controversies, which seem to keep her forever in the national conversation. Rollouts of partnerships,

> Today, Barbie is sold in more than 150 countries and represents a fifth of Mattel's business. Sales of Barbie products in 2022 reached nearly $1.5 billion.

fashion collections, new body shapes and skin colors all make the news, as do attacks by academics and feminists and pundits. Barbie herself has emerged as a social media star. As *New York* magazine put it in 2019, "Barbie's finally found her true calling: influencer."

That's not to say she hasn't stumbled. Product misfires include Barbie's 1997 friend Share-a-Smile Becky, who was disabled but whose wheelchair could not fit through the door of the Dreamhouse, and 2019's Dia De Muertos Barbie, whose face was adorned with traditional skull makeup and whose release prompted charges of cultural appropriation. There have been many tin-eared responses to criticism. Most gravely, there has been Barbie's failure to keep up with consumer tastes, which in the early 2000s began gravitating away from traditional toys and toward electronic games and then tablets. In 2009, Barbie's sales fell under $1 billion for the first time since 1992. She has regained ground in the last few years, especially following the introduction of the Fashionista line of curvy, petite, and tall Barbies, in 2016 and, of course, thanks to the recent buzz surrounding the *Barbie* movie. But she is still fending off popular competitors such as *Frozen*'s Elsa and the LOL Surprise! dolls, while trying to update her image with new careers and the Inspiring Women Series collection.

Barbie has always been critical to Mattel's success, and the Handlers fought aggressively to protect her. In the early 1960s, competitor Louis Marx uncovered Barbie's true origins as a sort of remake of Bild Lilli, and the company struck a deal with Greiner & Hausser, Bild Lilli's manufacturer. Hausser then applied for a U.S. patent for Bild Lilli's unique hip joint and licensed the patent to Marx. The arrangement allowed Marx to launch its own fashion doll, Miss Seventeen, and together the two companies sued Mattel in 1961 for copyright infringement and for copying Bild Lilli. Mattel denied it had knocked off Lilli. Rounds of charges and countercharges followed, and eventually the case was dismissed. Yet Mattel was the clear winner, as

Mattel's 2016 Barbie Fashionistas line introduced a variety of skin tones and body types (petite, tall, and curvy). "Yes, some people will say we are late to the game," Evelyn Mazzocco, then head of the Barbie brand, told TIME. "But changes at a huge corporation take time." Totally Hair Barbie (opposite), with her long, crimped locks, remains the company's best-seller.

Gerber pointed out in *Barbie and Ruth*: Following the litigation, the Handlers bought the rights to the Hausser patent for about $21,600.

Mattel not only gave birth to a new toy category with Barbie, it shaped the industry. The company bet on television, and its commercials were so successful, other toy companies followed suit. By advertising directly to consumers, manufacturers were able to change the power dynamic with retailers, gaining more leverage over the items that toy stores would stock.

Barbie kept on growing. In addition to sales of her endless stream of outfits, she also expanded

her circle of associates, with a boyfriend, Ken; a best friend, Midge; and a number of young relatives, not to mention her Dreamhouse, with elegant mid-century modern furnishings, multiple cars, and other accessories.

Rivals threatened, but Barbie has outlasted them all. First there was the Tammy doll, a wholesome-looking teenager from the Ideal Toy Company, which advertised her as "The Doll You Love to Dress." Tammy debuted in 1962, but by 1964 she was already off the market. In 1969, Ideal tried again, this time with Beautiful Crissy, a fashion doll whose auburn hair could be lengthened or shortened with the turn of a knob. There were several iterations of Crissy, including one who spoke, but by 1974 the line had run its course. Blythe, introduced by Kenner in 1972, had eyes that changed color; she lasted just one year. In the mid-'80s, Hasbro brought out a popular rocker doll, Jem, who worked during the day, performed at night, and soon found herself fighting with Rock Star Barbie for gigs.

THROUGH IT ALL, BARBIE SURVIVED multiple controversies, at least at the cash register. Perhaps the most infamous example was Teen Talk Barbie, whose catchphrases included "Math class is tough." Upon her release in 1992, a media firestorm erupted. A national association of math teachers wrote to Mattel with its objections, and a protest group calling itself the Barbie Liberation Organization swung into action. Buying Teen Talk Barbies and Talking Duke G.I. Joes from retailers around the country, the BLO removed the dolls' voice boxes. (The group claimed it was 300 dolls, but the number was unverifiable.) The activists then swapped the voice devices so that G.I. Joe twittered phrases such as "Let's plan our dream wedding!" and Barbie roared, "Attack!" "Vengeance is mine!" and "Eat lead, Cobra!" After repackaging the dolls, the BLO put them back on store shelves for unsuspecting consumers to buy and take home. When the operation came to light, media outlets covered it with barely veiled amusement. The *Washington Post* headline about the math teachers' objections to the talking doll was "Foot-in-Mouth Barbie." Meanwhile Barbie's popularity was undimmed. Sales that year remained above $1 billion, accounting for about half of Mattel's total.

Similarly, when Mattel teamed up with Nabisco and in 1997 introduced Oreo Fun Barbie, which came in both African American and Caucasian models, there was an outcry about the alternate, demeaning definition of Oreo—people of color who exhibit characteristics stereotypically associated with White people. Mattel discontinued Oreo Fun, and total Barbie sales in 1997 stayed steady at $1.7 billion.

As the '90s proceeded, Barbie seemed unstoppable. That lasted until 2001, when MGA Entertainment introduced four ethnically vague, bratty-looking teens who had, as the ads announced, "a passion for fashion." The first year Jade, Cloe, Yasmin, and Sasha—the Bratz—were on the market, they brought in sales of $97 million. By 2003, they had reached $1 billion, and by 2008, $3 billion. As MGA's fortunes soared, Barbie's sputtered. Between 2005 and 2006, Barbie-related revenues dropped by more than 12 percent.

Mattel sued MGA. MGA sued Mattel, and for more than a decade the two battled it out in court, with Mattel claiming it owned the design for dolls created by former Mattel employee Carter Bryant because his contract stipulated that anything he made while employed by Mattel belonged to Mattel. MGA claimed Mattel engaged in corporate espionage. In the end, it was a draw, with a federal appeals court in 2013 overturning a $172.5 million trade-secret award to MGA after already overturning Mattel's $100 million copyright verdict. The only money that changed hands went to the lawyers. Mattel was ordered to pay MGA $137 million in attorney fees and court costs.

Barbie was not Mattel's only problem child—or problem. In the wake of the Bratz debacle, sales of American Girl dolls, acquired by Mattel in 1998, started going into free fall in 2015. The popular-

Mattel's golden girl was as popular as ever in 2023. Margot Robbie and Ryan Gosling play Barbie and Ken (opposite) in the blockbuster Barbie, *directed by Greta Gerwig (above, third from left, with, from left, cast members Kate McKinnon, Issa Rae, Gosling, Robbie, America Ferrera, and Michael Cera).*

ity of Monster High dolls, an answer to the Bratz, also collapsed, and the Hot Wheels business flatlined. Then, in 2017, Mattel's second biggest customer, Toys"R"Us, filed for bankruptcy, and the trend that industry insiders call KGOY (kids getting older younger)—lingo for age compression, which shrinks the audience for toys—continued apace.

But Barbie and Mattel continue to fight to remain successful—and relevant. Mattel CEO Ynon Kreiz is capitalizing on the company's intellectual property in the mold of Hasbro, which has turned franchises such as Transformers and G.I. Joe into film successes. Barbie, of course, was the lynchpin of Kreiz's plan, and Mattel showed uncharacteristic restraint in allowing filmmaker Greta

Gerwig and star Margot Robbie to tell a story that didn't shy away from some of Barbie's problematic history. But first and foremost, the film—which exceeded lofty expectations with a $162 million opening weekend, the highest ever for a film with a female director—was a celebration of one of America's most enduring icons.

"What was so unique about what Greta did was she took a brand that has a strong purpose to inspire the limitless potential in every girl, and she took that message and broadened it and made it relevant and appealing to everyone," Kreiz told *Vanity Fair*. "We think this movie will recontextualize what people think of Barbie and what it represents to global audiences." ♥

The Woman Behind Barbie

RUTH HANDLER, THE CREATOR OF THE
MOST FAMOUS DOLL IN THE WORLD,
PLAYED A PIVOTAL PART IN THE MOVIE.

BY ELIANA DOCKTERMAN

WHEN GRETA GERWIG EMBARKED upon her journey to create a story about a doll with no personality or inner life, she turned to Barbie's history for inspiration. Mattel, Barbie's parent company, led the filmmaker through an "immersion" experience that outlined the iconic fashion doll's long history, from her debut in 1959 to her current status as the world's most recognizable toy, with over a billion dolls sold. Gerwig latched onto the relationship between Barbie's inventor, Ruth Handler, and Handler's daughter Barbara, for whom Barbie is named. "A Barbie movie is only ever going to be a mother-daughter movie on so many levels because it was Ruth Handler and Barbara—that was the relationship," the director told TIME.

And so Handler—who died in 2002 at age 85—had to be a part of the movie. She first appears as a mysterious woman in a 1950s-style kitchen tucked inside Mattel's headquarters.

"Barbie always represented the fact that a woman has choices," Handler (here in 1999) wrote in her 1994 autobiography, Dream Doll.

"If I had to stay home, I would be the most dreadful, mixed-up, unhappy woman in the world,"
Handler (with her husband, Elliot) told the Los Angeles Times *in 1959.*

Later, the film reveals that Handler is in fact the creator of Barbie and a godlike figure to Margot Robbie's character, one of many Barbies who resides in idyllic Barbie Land. Handler, played by *Cheers* alum Rhea Perlman, is presented as a kind yet imperfect deity.

Handler revolutionized the toy industry when she invented a mainstream doll with the proportions of an adult female. Before Barbie came along, girls mostly played with baby dolls, which conditioned them to be mothers. In the early 1950s, Handler had the rather forward-thinking idea that playing with dolls modeled on grown-up women would help girls imagine what they might be when they

grew up. Handler drew inspiration from her daughter, who would play dress-up with paper dolls.

Handler had already co-founded Mattel with her husband, Elliot, and Harold Matson in 1945 to sell picture frames before they pivoted to doll furniture and, eventually, other toys. But when she pitched the idea of an adult-looking doll to the company's executives, they balked: No mother, they argued, would buy their daughter a doll with breasts. The idea stalled until 1956 when, on a European vacation, Handler saw a German novelty doll called Bild Lilli in a store. The doll was based on a comic strip about a pinup with a voluptuous figure and was designed as a sexy trinket for soldiers during World

War II. Handler brought one of the dolls back to the U.S. to prove to Mattel's designers that they could produce something similar.

Barbie was unveiled at the 1959 Toy Fair in New York City, wearing the now iconic black-and-white striped bathing suit that Robbie dons in the opening scene of the film. The doll became a hit and buoyed Mattel to success. Fans clamored for Barbie to have a boyfriend, so Ken (named for Handler's son) was introduced in 1961. Barbie eventually transitioned from a fashion doll who played dress-up into a career woman who played dress-up as a doctor or astronaut. In her book *Forever Barbie: The Unauthorized Biography of a Real Doll*, author M.G. Lord argued that Barbie is the most potent icon of American culture in the late 20th century. "She's an archetypal female figure, she's something upon which little girls project their idealized selves," Lord wrote. "For most baby boomers, she has the same iconic resonance as any female saints, although without the same religious significance."

As *Barbie* hints, Ruth Handler was a complex woman. In 1978, she and several other Mattel executives were indicted by a federal grand jury for conspiracy, mail fraud, and giving the Securities and Exchange Commission false financial statements for the company. Handler pleaded no contest. She was fined $57,000 and sentenced to 2,500 hours of community service.

Handler had a second act in the 1980s selling a totally different product. During a scene in *Barbie,* Handler references her mastectomy, and the Barbie creator did indeed battle breast cancer. She saw a need for lifelike prostheses designed by and for women and sold a product called Nearly Me. She led a team of eight women, most of whom were breast cancer survivors, who would visit department stores and train sales staff to fit customers. Her sales tactics included what she called her "strip act," which involved removing her shirt to demonstrate that nobody could see or feel the difference between her real breast and her prosthesis.

> Handler had the rather forward-thinking idea that playing with dolls modeled on grown-up women would help girls imagine what they might be when they grew up.

People featured her in such a pose. She even fit first lady Betty Ford for a prosthesis after Ford's mastectomy. Handler eventually sold the company to Kimberly-Clark in the 1990s. Toward the end of her life, she reflected on her life as the inventor of an adult-shaped doll and a pioneer in prosthesis. According to the *Los Angeles Times*, she was fond of saying, "I've lived my life from breast to breast."

In the *Barbie* movie, the Ruth Handler role is a spiritual one. She shows up to comfort Barbie during a moment of existential crisis. She helps her escape the Mattel suits who want to put Barbie back in a box. At the time, Barbie doesn't know who this woman is, but it's clear they have a connection. Toward the end of the film, Ruth reveals her identity to Barbie, insisting that of course a woman was Barbie's original inventor—despite the fact that the Mattel boardroom is currently dominated by men. She cracks a joke about being beatific—referencing both her struggle with cancer and her money troubles with the government—and says that Barbie was designed not in the image of any one woman but to be aspirational. Barbie and Ruth have a conversation that echoes the heavenly train station moment in one of the Harry Potter films, in which Dumbledore helps Harry realize he has the option to live or die. Similarly, in a glowing space, a holy Ruth counsels Barbie on what it would mean to become fully human, face mortality, and leave Barbie Land to reside in the real world.

Ruth and Barbie touch hands twice in the movie, once over tea and again at the end of the film. Gerwig modeled the hand touch on the fresco of God giving life to Adam that appears on the ceiling of the Sistine Chapel. Here, Ruth as God instills life not in the first man but in woman—specifically a doll who has long been a symbol of what womanhood ought to be, for better or worse. When Barbie leaves Barbie Land, she is leaving a matriarchal version of Eden to enter a much messier real world. It turns out, in *Barbie* anyway, that God is a woman, and a rather complicated one at that. ❤

The Barbie Judge Doll was born in 2019.

Barbie's Many Careers

THROUGH THE DECADES,
BARBIE STEPPED OUT
OF HER PLASTIC BOX
AND SHATTERED THE
GLASS CEILING.

BY COURTNEY MIFSUD INTREGLIA

1965
ASTRONAUT
Years before man stepped on the moon, Miss Astronaut Barbie unveiled her Project Mercury–style spacesuit.

1973
SURGEON
When Barbie donned her surgical mask, women made up about 5 percent of all physicians in the United States.

1990
AIR FORCE BARBIE
The doll debuted just before Air Force pilot Lisa Wilson became the first enlisted woman to fly in combat.

1992
PRESIDENT
Since 1992, Barbie has run for president in every election year, with running mates included in later iterations.

1996
VETERINARIAN
With dog and cat patients included, this Barbie also came with a device that made various animal sounds.

1994
FIREFIGHTER
Now an emergency responder, Firefighter Barbie came with a rescue bag and a dalmatian fire dog.

1998
WOMEN'S WORLD CUP
This soccer-themed Barbie celebrated Mia Hamm, a star forward on the United States women's national team.

1998
NASCAR DRIVER
Barbie put the pedal to the metal to celebrate the 50th annversary of NASCAR with an authentic racing uniform.

2002
ART TEACHER
Little sister Kelly learned about art from Barbie and even wore a matching outfit. The set came with supplies to create real-world art projects.

2009
NEWBORN BABY DOCTOR
Barbie entered the hospital yet again. This time she came with newborn twin babies and a fully furnished nursery.

2010
NEWS ANCHOR
This journalist Barbie doll came with a code inside each package that unlocked career-themed content online.

2011
ARCHITECT
In 2010, Mattel had the public vote on Barbie's next career. The following year, Architect Barbie was unveiled.

2012
YOGA INSTRUCTOR
This career iteration created some online buzz and controversy for including a dog instead of more yoga-centric props.

**2016
PRESIDENTIAL CANDIDATES**
*In this election year,
Mattel unveiled an all-
female ticket of Barbie
and her running mate.*

2016
GAME DEVELOPER
As a departure from Barbie's signature glam, Mattel aimed to create an "industry-inspired" design with realistic gear.

2018
ROBOT ENGINEER
Designed to interest girls in STEM jobs, this Barbie came with a robot that could be bent and reconfigured.

2019
BASKETBALL PLAYER
This Barbie had 22 "joints" throughout her body so that she could be moved to represent an athletic range of motion.

2021
SPACE DISCOVERY
Two of these Barbies were launched aboard a rocket in 2022 and spent months on the International Space Station.

Boy Toy

THE HISTORY OF BARBIE'S
MOST FAMOUS ACCESSORY: KEN.

BY SHANNON CARLIN

N THE *BARBIE* MOVIE, Ken is just Ken. But who is Ken—or, perhaps the better question is, *why* is Ken? He is not the peanut butter to Barbie's jelly. No, he's the neon-pink plate that Barbie would use while eating an impeccably made PB&J.

Ken is a piece of delicious but wholly unnecessary arm candy for Barbie, a woman who can do it all on her own. For the last 64 years, she has been doing just that: holding down more than 200 jobs, including Air Force pilot, robotics engineer, baby doctor, Mars explorer, and president, putting other famous multi-hyphenates to shame. All Barbie's boyfriend does, according to Greta Gerwig's film, is "beach," which, as Barbie's über Ken, Ryan Gosling, noted throughout the movie's press tour, is a difficult occupation to define, and certainly not one to brag about. This might be why Gosling's Ken is in the midst of an existential crisis. (Listen to Ken's blond fragility ballad "I'm Just Ken" to understand how deep the prototypical himbo's inferiority complex runs—or, should we say, skates.)

Barbie's plus one has finally realized something the rest of us have known forever: It's Barbie's world, and he's just living in it.

Kenneth Sean Carson hit store shelves in March 1961, two years after Mattel released the first Barbie doll. Ken was created as a male counterpart and companion to Barbie by Ruth Handler, the inventor of the iconic mononymous fashion doll, in response to those who wrote to Mattel complaining about Barbie's singledom. "Ken was invented after Barbie, to burnish Barbie's position in our eyes and in the world," Gerwig told *Vogue*. "That kind of creation myth is the opposite of the creation myth in Genesis."

Ken is 12 inches tall, which is half an inch taller than Barbie. Handler and designer Charlotte Johnson wanted Ken to stand out from Barbie in other ways as well. The two advocated for Ken to have some sort of genitalia, "if no actual penis, then at least a 'bulge' in his trousers," according to *Esquire*. "The squeamish male executives at Mattel" did not agree; Ken's smooth groin area was the compromise the two parties reached. The first Ken doll wore a red bathing suit and cork sandals, despite looking as if he hadn't spent much time in the sun. His hair, which came in blond and brunette, was initially

The 2023 version of Ken, based on his movie look, features a denim ensemble.

1961
The first Ken had felt hair (a choice of two colors) and was ready for the beach.

1978
Superstar Ken was decked out in velour and ready to boogie during the disco era.

1984
Dream Date Ken was, as Mattel put it, "the perfect arm candy for Barbie."

1992
Totally Hair Ken came with a tube of gel to complete the '90s vibe.

made of flocked felt, but once Mattel realized that Ken's hair would fall off when wet, they replaced it, in 1962, with a molded plastic style. He got upgraded to rooted, or synthetic, hair in 1973.

Since Ken's release, he has had more than 100 different looks that, more often than not, perfectly complement Barbie's. Ken debuted the blond hair and tanned physique that would become his trademark in 1979 with the release of Sun Lovin' Malibu Ken, whose aqua swim trunks hide his tan lines. Three years later, Mattel came out with the first African American Ken doll, but it wasn't until 2021 that the company released its most diverse line of Kens. To mark his 60th anniversary, Mattel

offered Kens with a range of skin tones, body types, abilities, and man buns.

Ken has held nearly 40 jobs in his 62 years: astronaut, hamburger chef, country-western singer, and lifeguard, to name but a few. His most common occupation? Twelve Kens have held the not-so-flattering job title of "beach bum." Perhaps Ken's questionable employment is why he has never procured a Dreamhouse of his own. He did finally get his own car in 2012: a red Mini Cooper with a set of vanity license plates ("Ken").

Ken was named after Kenneth Handler, the son of Ruth and Elliot Handler. The original Ken always claimed he was nothing like his namesake

2010

Accept no substitutes: In recent years, Mattel has packaged some of the dolls with a "Genuine Ken" wrist tag.

2017

Ken joined the Barbie Fashionistas line with 15 new dolls, featuring three body types and seven skin tones.

that despite thinking Barbie was "a bimbo," he got such a "kick" out of seeing little girls line up outside his mother-in-law's Wyoming home in 1963 to meet the real Ken. "They were so sweet and so terrific," he said. "It was so important to them."

ACCORDING TO MATTEL, KEN AND Barbie met in 1961 while filming their first commercial together. It was love at first sight, and the two, who both hail from the (fictional) town of Willows, Wisconsin, started going steady. But in the 2000s, things got a little more complicated for the couple. After more than 40 years of dating, the duo consciously uncoupled. "Like other celebrity couples, their Hollywood romance has come to an end," Russell Arons, then vice president of marketing at Mattel, said in a 2004 statement. Barbie and Ken felt it was "time to spend some quality time apart," with Arons hinting that Ken's reluctance to put a ring on it may have played a part in their breakup. Still, the two swore the split was amicable and that they would remain friends. Barbie went on to date a hip-hop-loving Australian boogie boarder named Blaine.

Two years after they called it quits, Ken attempted to win Barbie back by getting a makeover. "Ken has revamped his life—mind, body, and soul," Hollywood stylist and Mattel consultant Phillip Bloch said in 2006. "Everyone knows how difficult it is to change, especially when you've lived your life a certain way for more than four decades." Barbie's then publicist, Lauren Dougherty, said her client appreciated Ken's effort but that fans would "have to stay tuned to see whether these two will get back together."

On Valentine's Day 2011, Mattel announced that the couple had reunited after rekindling their romance on the set of *Toy Story 3*. "As we like to put it, they found they were kind of missing each other," Lisa McKnight, vice president of marketing at Mattel, told *Entertainment Weekly*. "They had a lot of fun together. Now a little time has passed since the shoot and all the premiere noise around the movie and all that good stuff, and I think they both realized that they're made for each other." The couple are still together today but don't appear to have any plans to settle down and start a

toy. "Ken doll is Malibu," he told the *Los Angeles Times* in 1989. "He goes to the beach and surfs. He is all these perfect American things." As a teen, the real Ken "played the piano and went to movies with subtitles. I was a nerd—a real nerd," he explained. "All the girls thought I was a jerk."

According to the 2009 book *Toy Monster: The Big, Bad World of Mattel*, Jerry Oppenheimer's unauthorized look at the company's history and corporate approach, Handler reportedly "grew up embarrassed and humiliated by having an anatomically incorrect boy doll named after him . . . [with] no hint of genitalia." However, Ken Handler, who died of a brain tumor in 1994, told the *Los Angeles Times*

family. The *New York Times Magazine* noted that the fact "that Barbie has never had a child remains one of the most radical things about her."

ARRING MAGIC KEN, RELEASED IN MAY 1993, is considered to be the most famous Ken doll—and one of the most controversial. The platinum-blond-streaked Ken, who, yes, sported a silver hoop earring was "a big breakthrough," Lisa McKendall, then the manager of communications for Mattel, told the *New York Times*. "We never would have done this a few years ago. But now you see more earrings on men. They are more accepted in day-to-day life. We are trying to keep Ken updated."

At the time, author and journalist Dan Savage compared Ken's new cool-guy look—a purple pleather vest worn over a lavender mesh top with black jeans—to "three-year-old rave wear," writing in the Seattle altweekly *The Stranger* that Mattel "spent a weekend in L.A. or New York dashing from rave to rave, taking notes and Polaroids" for inspiration. What did catch Savage's eye, though, was Ken's necklace, which to him (and many others) looked like a certain sex toy. "It's a necklace. It holds charms he can share with Barbie," McKendall said when Savage asked about Earring Magic Ken's possibly erotic jewelry. "C'mon, this is a doll designed for little girls. Something like that would be entirely inappropriate."

Savage argued that Mattel had given the world "Queer Ken." (The first openly LGBTQ+ doll, Gay Bob, was released in 1977.) The company told him that was not their intention. "Ken and Barbie both reflect mainstream society, reflect what little girls see in their world," McKendall said. "What they see their dads, brothers, and uncles wearing, they want Ken to wear." However, in 2021, former Mattel employee Carol Spencer told *Mel* magazine that at the time, the designers of the doll were well aware that Ken's more flamboyant look would lead some to question his sexuality. "I do recall the male Mattel designer—who was married with several children

and working on the project—saying to me: 'They will turn Ken gay with this doll!'"

Mattel discontinued Earring Magic Ken after six months, but the doll became particularly popular with LGBTQ+ collectors. It is said to be the best-selling Ken doll in Mattel's history. (Mattel has seemingly disowned the controversial doll; it's not listed on Barbie's official online archive, which makes it difficult to fact-check the claims of its popularity.) Of course, this only adds to the lore of Ken and his magic earring. After 30 years, in 2022, *Dazed* declared that Gosling's *Barbie* look "represents the ultimate vindication of Magic Earring Ken," who has become a symbol of LGBTQ+ pride and brand failure.

As for the most infamous Ken doll, that would be Sugar Daddy Ken. Released in 2010, the $82 doll was part of the Barbie Collector line aimed at adults, and, according to Mattel, "exemplifies fantastic Palm Beach fashion." This Ken is significantly older than his predecessors—check out his gray coif!—and much more dapper, with his preppy lime-green jacquard blazer, pink polo, and white pleated slacks. His look was inspired by photographer Slim Aarons' "Palm Beach Party" images, which often featured tanned socialites hanging out in the South Florida town. But it's Sugar Daddy Ken's little white terrier that completes his look. Despite what some may think, Mattel said this Ken's name was not a reference to older wealthy men who take up with younger lovers but to his dog companion, Sugar. He's Sugar's daddy, get it? Most people didn't, which might be why Gerwig chose to enlist this particular Ken (played by Rob Brydon) for a very funny *Barbie* cameo.

Thanks to Barbie, Ken has been given a major glow-up. Gosling is just one of many actors who gets to show off his "Ken-ergy," a fitting term for the mysterious aura each Ken possesses. Simu Liu, Ncuti Gatwa, Kingsley Ben-Adir, and Scott Evans are also members of the film's Ken-munity. (Michael Cera plays Ken's mostly forgotten BFF, Allan.) Gosling and Liu got dolls made in their Barbie like-

> Ken has been given a major glow-up. Ryan Gosling is just one of many actors who gets to show off his "Ken-ergy," a fitting term for the mysterious aura each Ken possesses.

Sugar Daddy Ken (or as Mattel tried to explain, "Sugar's Daddy, Ken"—the dog's name was Sugar) was released in 2010, to considerable eye-rolling. The character made a brief cameo in Barbie.

nesses that some have argued don't look that much like them. While not a total Ken-tastrophe, it does feel like par for the course when it comes to the doll that has always been an afterthought.

But Gosling seems hell-bent on changing the world's opinion of Ken, launching a one-man #JusticeForKen campaign in the lead-up to the movie's release. He told *GQ* that while contemplating whether he would sign on to do *Barbie,* he actually found his daughters' Ken doll "face down in the mud outside one day, next to a squished lemon, and

it was like, 'This guy's story does need to be told,' you know?" He's spoken out against the hypocrisy that popped up online after some argued that he was too old to play Ken. "Suddenly, it's like, 'No, we've cared about Ken this whole time,'" Gosling said about the #NotMyKen movement. "If you ever really cared about Ken, you would know that nobody cared about Ken. So your hypocrisy is exposed. This is why his story must be told." With *Barbie,* Gosling attempts to do the impossible: Prove that while Ken certainly isn't Barbie, he's always been Ken-ough. ♥

CHAPTER

2

Bringing Barbie to Life

BY FINDING THE HUMANITY IN A PLASTIC
DOLL, DIRECTOR GRETA GERWIG CREATED
A SMART, FUNNY ADVENTURE THAT
BECAME AN UNLIKELY BLOCKBUSTER.

Gerwig (center) with members of her cast: Margot Robbie, Alexandra Shipp, Michael Cera, America Ferrera, and Ariana Greenblatt.

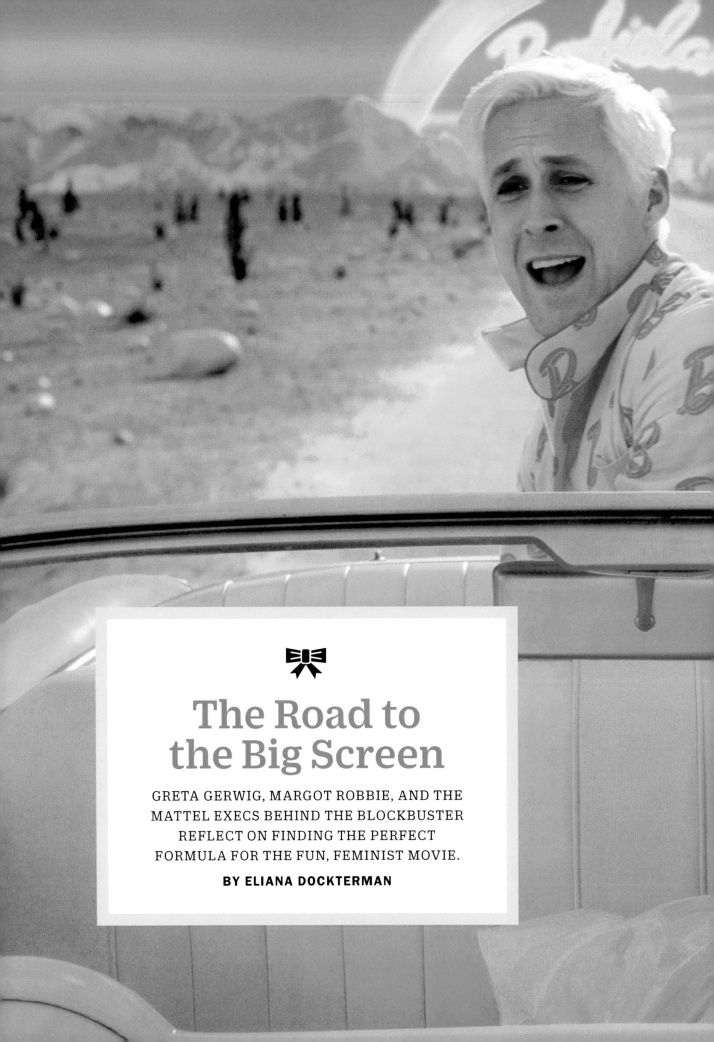

The Road to the Big Screen

GRETA GERWIG, MARGOT ROBBIE, AND THE
MATTEL EXECS BEHIND THE BLOCKBUSTER
REFLECT ON FINDING THE PERFECT
FORMULA FOR THE FUN, FEMINIST MOVIE.

BY ELIANA DOCKTERMAN

On their journey to the real world, Ken and Barbie belt out "Closer to Fine," the Indigo Girls' 1989 anthem of self-discovery.

Greta Gerwig (with laptop) on set with a trio of her Barbies: Margot Robbie (Stereotypical Barbie), Ana Cruz Kayne (Judge Barbie), and Hari Nef (Doctor Barbie).

THERE'S PLENTY TO consider about Barbie, but let's start with her feet. Perfectly arched, but not quite demi-pointe—the ideal position to fit into any pump. They're instantly recognizable to anyone who has ever played with the iconic doll. So when the trailer for the *Barbie* movie opened with a shot of star Margot Robbie stepping out of Barbie's marabou stilettos, still on tiptoes, the internet exploded. On TikTok, people attempted to mimic the viral shot with their highest heels. The *Wall Street Journal* interviewed a podiatrist about the physical impossibility of the moment. "I need to know everything," tweeted Chrissy Teigen.

Robbie has answers: The shot took eight takes. She had to hold onto a bar to keep her feet flexed. And yes, those are her feet. "I really don't like it when someone else does my hands or feet in an insert shot," she says.

Playing Barbie is complicated, and not just because it requires immense calf strength. I've reported on Barbie's parent company, Mattel, for the better part of a decade and sat in on test groups with moms and their kids. Some parents say Barbie inspires their children to imagine themselves as an astronaut or politician. But others refuse to buy the doll—with her tiny waist and large breasts—because she has set an impossible beauty standard for their daughters, a problem that precipitated major changes to her look in 2016. A Barbie movie was always going to be fraught, and the studio marketing the film knows it. As the trailer posits, "If you love Barbie, this movie is for you. If you hate Barbie, this movie is for you."

Robbie adds, "If you feel indifferent about Barbie or haven't thought about Barbie in years, this movie is also for you."

The scene-stealing Kate McKinnon (with Gosling) is Weird Barbie, who's been "played with a little too hard."

When it was announced in 2021 that Greta Gerwig, who directed the Oscar-nominated coming-of-age films *Lady Bird* and *Little Women*, would helm *Barbie*, fans were confused, surprised, and delighted. Maybe the movie would be an idiosyncratic, subversive, even feminist take on the doll, not just a commercial for Mattel. But like Barbie herself, the movie's existence is an exercise in contradictions.

Before the film opened to record-breaking numbers, many wondered whether *Barbie* would be a satire of a toy company's capitalist ambitions, a searing indictment of the current fraught state of gender relations, a heartwarming if occasionally clichéd tribute to girl power, or a musical spectacle filled with earworms from Nicki Minaj and Dua Lipa. The answer, it turned out, was all of the above. And then some.

It was the most anticipated movie of the summer of 2023—if not the entire year—which means a lot was riding on *Barbie*. Not just for Robbie and Gerwig, neither of whom has ever produced a movie on this scale, but also for Mattel. After a period of declining sales, a recently reinvigorated Barbie was ready for her big-screen debut. Barbie's move to Hollywood is the brainchild of Mattel CEO Ynon Kreiz, who came into the job five years ago with a vision to leverage the company's intellectual property into a cinematic universe based on Mattel toys.

Barbie was the proof of concept when it hit theaters on July 21, scoring $162 million at the domestic box office on its opening weekend and reaching $1 billion in global ticket sales in just 17 days. Anything associated with the film—a rare blockbuster catering directly to women—

was breathlessly received, from paparazzi photos of Robbie and co-star Ryan Gosling (as Ken) skating down Venice Beach in fluorescent spandex a year before the film's release to an early teaser that cleverly parodied *2001: A Space Odyssey*. Mattel engineered some of the hype by launching Malibu Barbie cafés and announcing partnerships with Bloomingdale's, Crocs, and Hot Topic. Other moments suggested a snowball effect: Kim Kardashian threw her daughter a Barbie-themed birthday party, and celebs were seen stepping out in hot pink designer minidresses.

Just ahead of the film's release, Gerwig still couldn't seem to believe she got away with making this version. "This movie is a goddamn miracle," she says. She calls it a "surprising spicy margarita." By the time you realize the salted rim has cayenne mixed in, it's too late: "You can already taste the sweetness, and you sort of go with the spice."

H OW DID A FILMMAKER WHO IS BEST known for thoughtful movies about women's inner lives come to write and direct a movie about a toy who has no inner life and is (mostly) defined by her looks? It's simple: Gerwig loves dolls. "I played with dolls too long," says the 40-year-old director. "I was still doing it in junior high. Kids were drinking, and I was playing with dolls." Gerwig's mom wasn't a fan of Barbie for feminist reasons: "She went through the '60s and was like, 'What did we do all this for?'" But playing with Barbies proved to be a training ground for Gerwig's job as a professional storyteller.

Gerwig and her partner, the filmmaker Noah Baumbach, wrote the script under unusual circumstances. After they participated in a Barbie boot camp put on by Mattel, which began with a history lesson on Barbie inventor Ruth Handler and involved a tour of Barbie's most fabulous (and regrettable) fashions, the pandemic struck. Cloistered in their home in New York City, the duo didn't receive typical studio notes as they drafted. "We worked hard to give them their space and let them come up with what the movie was going to be, uninterrupted, without people pushing an agenda on them—not Mattel, not Warner Bros., not us," says Robbie, whose company LuckyChap Entertainment co-produced the film. "And then when I saw the script, I was like, 'They're never going to let us do this. This is really pushing it.'"

Barbie is a fun yet self-aware romp with shades of *Clueless* and *Legally Blonde*. It's also stuffed full of ideas and occasionally overwhelmed by them. The movie is set in Barbie Land, a utopia where each Barbie has an impressive job. As Helen Mirren's narrator wryly tells us, "all problems of feminism and equal rights have been solved." The Barbies have sleepovers every night during which they declare how beautiful and confident they feel. The Kens (played by Gosling and Simu Liu, among others) exist as convenient dance partners. But then Robbie's Barbie begins to think about mortality. Those arched feet go flat. Cellulite appears on her thigh. To combat these changes, she ventures into the real world with Ken, who has been feeling like a mere accessory in Barbie's dream life. The real world is, well, real. Men in suits at Mattel—led by Will Ferrell's CEO—make disingenuous speeches about female empowerment; preteens dress Barbie down for wreaking havoc on their self-esteem. Both Barbie and Ken go on quests of self-discovery. And that's when things get *really* interesting.

There's also a surprisingly balletic musical number that appears to be inspired by *Grease* and *Singin' in the Rain*; a car-chase sequence; a mysterious woman in a kitchen (who turns out to be Handler); and a running gag about Sylvester Stallone's penchant for mink coats.

Every single actor TIME spoke to cited Gerwig and the sharp script as the reason they joined the film. "I knew this was not going to shy away from the parts of Barbie that are more interesting but potentially a little bit more fraught," says Hari Nef, who plays Doctor Barbie. "The contemporary history of feminism and body positivity—there are questions of how Barbie can fit into all of that."

Those points proved more controversial with the corporate entities involved. Robbie Brenner, the first-ever executive producer of Mattel Films and the architect of its cinematic universe, told the company's top brass, "You're just gonna white-knuckle it the whole time."

Gerwig earned the toymaker's trust with the help of Robbie. At one point, Richard Dickson, then COO and president of Mattel, says he flew to the London set to argue with Gerwig and Robbie over a particular scene involving how Barbie affects girls' self-esteem, which he felt was off brand. Dickson dials up his natural boyish exuberance, imitating himself righteously marching off the plane to meet them. But Gerwig and Robbie performed the scene for him and changed his mind. "When you look on the page, the nuance isn't there, the delivery isn't there," Robbie explains.

Robbie had laid the groundwork for this with Mattel's CEO when she met with him in 2018 in the hopes that LuckyChap could take on the *Barbie* project. "In that very first meeting, we impressed upon Ynon that we are going to honor the legacy of your brand, but if we don't acknowledge certain things—if we don't say it, someone else is going to say it," she says. "So you might as well be a part of that conversation."

KREIZ WAS THE FOURTH MATTEL CEO in four years when he took over in 2018. He orchestrated a turnaround that included courting Hollywood's biggest talent with an exacting pitch that has proved persuasive. "It's not about making movies so that we can go and sell more toys," he says. "We've been doing well selling toys without movies." (The movie does help: The day a Margot Robbie Barbie went on sale, it became the No. 1 doll on Amazon.) "The most important transition was from being a toy-manufacturing company that was making items to becoming an IP company that is managing franchises," Kreiz continues. It's a particularly prescient strategy at a moment when superhero fatigue has set in and studios are desperate to find new intellectual property with a built-in fan base, from Super Mario Bros. to Dungeons & Dragons. Mattel has announced 14 more movies based on its toys, including a J.J. Abrams–produced Hot Wheels movie and (intriguingly) a Barney film with Daniel Kaluuya. The expansion also includes more streaming shows, video games, and a Mattel theme park currently under construction in Arizona.

Before Kreiz hired Brenner as executive producer of Mattel Films, he asked who she thought should play the iconic doll. She, too, said Robbie. "She's very funny, she's deep, she's a fantastic actress, and she does look like…" Brenner pauses. "She's beautiful."

> "If [Mattel] hadn't made that change to have a multiplicity of Barbies, I don't think I would have wanted to attempt to make a Barbie film."
>
> –MARGOT ROBBIE

It's obvious why both executives zeroed in on Robbie. She does look like Barbie. Or, as the film says, she looks like Stereotypical Barbie. The distinction is important. Just eight years back, in 2015, Barbie's sales had sunk to $900 million, the lowest in 25 years. So in 2016, Mattel made the biggest change to the doll since her debut. After rolling out a wider array of skin tones and hair types for the dolls, Mattel launched three new body types, including a curvy Barbie. It (eventually) worked. Barbie sales rose and hit a record $1.7 billion in 2021 before a small industry-wide slump last year.

Mattel had been toying with the idea of a Barbie movie since 2009. Big stars (Amy Schumer, Anne Hathaway) and prominent directors like Patty Jenkins were rumored to be attached before Robbie met with the company in 2018. One of the reasons Mattel resisted bringing Barbie to the big screen for so long was that the company had worked hard to modernize the brand and establish that Barbie is not one body, one personality, one woman. There are currently 175 different Barbies, with different combinations of body shape, skin tone, and hair type. And yet, there is Margot Robbie on the poster as the manifestation of Barbie. There's a moment in the film where Mirren makes a tongue-in-cheek joke about Robbie being too beautiful to feel insecure.

Dickson argues that Barbie had to look like Robbie to get audience members who perhaps haven't followed Mattel's latest updates into theaters. "Of course she looks like Barbie," he says. "But they're all Barbie. It's the perfect cast to express what Barbie is today. And Margot is the bridge."

Robbie is flattered that the Mattel execs thought of her, but she would never have wanted to play the only Barbie. "If [Mattel] hadn't made that change to have a multiplicity of Barbies, I don't think I would have wanted to attempt to make a Barbie film," she says. "I don't think you should say, 'This is the one version of what Barbie is, and that's what women should aspire to be and look like and act like.'"

Issa Rae, who plays President Barbie, argues that

"Everyone in Barbie Land is a perfect Barbie," Issa Rae (President Barbie) told Glamour. *"I found that so beautiful. Almost everyone in the world is represented in some way here."*

the entire point of the film is to portray a world in which there isn't a singular ideal. "My worry was that it was going to feel too white feminist–y, but I think that it's self-aware," she says. "Barbie Land is perfect, right? It represents perfection. So if perfection is just a bunch of white Barbies, I don't know that anybody can get on board with that."

But it seems Mattel was resistant to appearing too modern. "It was a matter of finding the right talent that can appreciate the brand's authenticity and bring that controversy to life in a way that, yes, pokes fun at us but ultimately is purposeful and has heart," says Dickson.

Still, in an interview with TIME, Brenner called Gerwig's film "not a feminist movie," a sentiment echoed by other Mattel executives. It was a striking contrast to conversations with many of the actors, who used that term unprompted to describe the script. When Mattel's words are relayed to Robbie, she raises an eyebrow. "Who said that?" she asks, then sighs. "It's not that it is or it isn't. It's a

movie. It's a movie that's got so much in it." The bigger point, Robbie impresses upon me, is "we're in on the joke. This isn't a Barbie puff piece."

B ARBIE'S CORVETTE ISN'T ANY OLD convertible with a slick of pink paint. If you place the doll in her car, it's too small—the windshield ends at her chest. And so Gerwig insisted the life-size version must be a little small for Robbie. Barbie's vehicle was carefully created as a model and then scaled up using a mathematical formula to ensure everything in Barbie Land looked "toyetic."

Gerwig's team built an entire neighborhood made up of Dreamhouses that were missing walls. The skies and clouds in the background were hand-painted to render a playroom-like quality, as was much of the rest of the set. "From a production perspective, it's bigger than anything we've done before," says Tom Ackerley, Robbie's producing partner and husband. "We wanted it to feel like you could reach into the screen and touch it."

CONTINUED ON PAGE 58

On the way to the real world, the impeccably dressed Barbie and Ken stop for a quick cookout.

CONTINUED FROM PAGE 55

LuckyChap enlisted David Heyman, who produced the Harry Potter films, to help create this fantastical world. "I don't think we have seen or will ever see a film with more pink in it," says Heyman. Gerwig jokingly nicknamed the duo Ken David and Ken Tom.

Not everyone in the film had as robust a relationship with Barbie growing up as Gerwig did. Kate McKinnon, for example, preferred to play with shells she found on the beach or small plastic zoo animals. "I didn't see myself in Barbie when I was younger," says the *SNL* alum. "I saw myself in an inflatable lobster." But McKinnon watched her sister and her friends play with the dolls: They cut Barbie's hair, drew on her face, and even set her on fire. She theorizes, "They were externalizing how they felt, and they felt different." So when Gerwig offered McKinnon the role of Weird Barbie, a doll that's been played with a little too aggressively in the real world, she jumped at the chance. McKinnon was impressed by the way the script dealt with girls' complicated attachment to the doll. "It comments honestly about the positive and negative feelings," she says. "It's an incisive cultural critique."

Alexandra Shipp, who plays an Author Barbie, also projected onto the dolls as a child. Shipp rode on Warner Bros.' Barbie float in the West Hollywood Pride parade this year and reflects that Barbie helped her explore aspects of her identity. "When you're a kid, your toys are an extension of who you are and how you can exist in the world as an adult," she says. "Sure, I had Kens, but when I played house, I had two Barbies raising a Skipper."

On social media, Nef published a letter she wrote to Gerwig and Robbie asking to play one of the Barbies in the film. She says that as a trans woman, she feels ambivalent about the word *doll*, a slang term in queer culture for trans women, particularly those who celebrate the high femme. The word can feel at once aspirational and oppressive. "It's a tricky word that holds, for me, anyway, such a strict standard created by the patriarchy that deserves to be scrutinized, but also a promise of liberation and safety and belonging," Nef says. "At the very least, there's a juicy performance as a doll somewhere in there."

T HE WORLD MAY BE OBSESSED WITH Barbie's feet, but Gerwig would like to draw attention to Barbie's hands. While holed up in New York putting the final touches on the movie, the director was eager to dig into its mi-

nutiae. She points out that there is a specific image in the film that bears a striking resemblance to Michelangelo's "The Creation of Adam." She starts to point a finger downward, excitedly mimicking the moment in which God bestows life on the first man. Except in Gerwig's filmed fresco, Barbie creator Ruth Handler's hand touches Barbie's hand. "It's on the same trajectory and angle as the Sistine Chapel," she says. "Nobody is going to notice that, so I have to say it." There's a lot to unpack in the notion of Handler, as God, creating the perfect woman, to be placed in an idyllic matriarchy—and the inevitable chaos that will ensue when Barbie leaves this paradise. But any time I get too deep into references or the politics of the film with Gerwig or the actors, I'm quickly reminded by an executive or a producer that it's a fun summer romp.

And it is, in part. It's a mash-up of corporate

When Robbie's Barbie reveals that her feet have fallen flat, the other Barbies (Ana Cruz Kayne, Sharon Rooney, Alexandra Shipp, Hari Nef, and Emma Mackey) are horrified.

ambition and personal quirk. Perhaps that's a triumph in an era when movies about products are en vogue. In 2023 alone we've seen films based on a Nike shoe (*Air*), an obsolete smartphone (*Black-Berry*), and even a snack (*Flamin' Hot*). For Mattel, *Barbie* is just the beginning. Kreiz enthuses about the possibility of more Barbie movies.

Robbie hedges. "It could go a million different directions from this point," she says. "But I think you fall into a bit of a trap if you try and set up a first movie whilst also planning for sequels."

It's hard to imagine a sequel, or any other toy movie for that matter, making the splash that *Barbie* has. "We're looking to create movies that become cultural events," Kreiz says, and to do that, Mattel needs visionaries to produce something more intriguing than a toy ad. "If you can excite filmmakers like Greta and Noah to embrace the opportunity and have creative freedom, you can have a real impact."

Gerwig herself admits that "sometimes these movies can have a quality of hegemonic capitalism," and that she had to find ways to make the movie her own. She wove in footage of the cast and crew's friends and family, including images Robbie had filmed herself on a Super 8 over the years, to give the film a personal touch. It's a home movie smack-dab in the heart of a summer blockbuster, and Gerwig cries every time she watches that part. "It's like sneaking in humanity to something that everybody thinks is a hunk of plastic," she says. ♥

Margot Steps Out

FOR THE *BARBIE* PRESS TOUR, ROBBIE WORKED WITH STYLIST ANDREW MUKAMAL TO PAY TRIBUTE TO THE DOLL'S OUTFITS FROM DIFFERENT ERAS.

BY CADY LANG

1. For a Seoul press conference, Robbie wore an embellished dress and jacket set from Moschino and carried a matching quilted purse.
2. At the Los Angeles photo-call, she donned a Valentino polka-dot skirt suit with a halter neck.
3. Mukamal commissioned the haute-couture house Schiaparelli to re-create the Solo in the Spotlight Barbie dress for the L.A. premiere.
4. The Pucci minidress Robbie wore for a photo-call in Mexico City was a nod to Totally Hair Barbie.
5. & 6. Robbie did a double play for the Seoul premiere, evoking Day-to-Night Barbie: day, Atelier Versace fuchsia skirt suit with white accents; night, a party dress iwith a full tulle skirt in the same fuchsia shade.
7. At a London photo-call, she wore a Vivienne Westwood jacket styled with a corseted miniskirt.
8. The London premiere was an homage to Enchanted Evening Barbie: a corseted pink Vivienne Westwood gown.

Dreaming Up Barbie Land

HOW GRETA GERWIG AND HER TEAM
GOT EVERYTHING—FROM THE CLOTHES
TO THE SETS—JUST RIGHT.

BY ELIANA DOCKTERMAN

The Dreamhouses "defy architectural logic," production designer Sarah Greenwood told People, and they required behind-the-scenes magic to stay upright.

**ARBIE** IS A MOVIE THAt benefits from multiple screenings. On every viewing, you'll catch something different, whether it's a big idea or a tiny detail. When the film hit theaters on July 21, every person who has ever dressed up a Barbie was bound to recognize some outfit or prop from their childhood, whether they played with the doll in the 1960s or 1990s. Even the Barbie-agnostic could find something to pick up on, whether it was references to the Technicolor musicals of Old Hollywood or a famous scene from *The Matrix*.

Filmed primarily at a studio in London, the story of *Barbie* begins in a pink wonderland called Barbie Land, where sexism doesn't exist. The Barbies celebrate their good fortune with nightly slumber parties. It's a lived-in fantasy world that relies primarily on physical sets rather than CGI. To build out Barbie Land, writer-director Greta Gerwig decided to create a coherent set of rules that would govern how it looked and functioned. In order to do that, she dove into the history of Barbie, the history of movies, and the history of fashion.

Back in 2018 and 2019, Gerwig, star Margot Robbie, and folks from Robbie's production company LuckyChap Entertainment went through an immersion course designed by Mattel. The unofficial Barbie boot camp began with the doll's origin story— Barbie was created by Ruth Handler—and took a tour through some of Barbie's best outfits over the years. This research served as inspiration for the story. Gerwig and filmmaker Noah Baumbach, her co-writer and life partner, also had to build a world from scratch. "You see a seamless universe that all makes sense, and that's because there were these very specific boundaries about what could and couldn't happen," says Kate McKinnon, who plays one of the Barbies. One such rule? Barbie Land is a utopia, so nothing can be cluttered. There is no trash. "Nothing is dirty in the world, even when it gets its most chaotic," says McKinnon. "I was struck by that."

Given that Barbie first came to market in 1959, Gerwig and Oscar-nominated production designer Sarah Greenwood decided to run with a mid-century modern aesthetic for Barbie's Dreamhouse and many of her fashions. Barbie lives on the sort of suburban cul de sac idealized in that era. The Dreamhouses were built without walls, so the actors had to be attached to wires so they didn't topple off the top floor of their home when they got out of bed. But the cast says everything else in their Dreamhouses was surprisingly functional: They would sit on the retro chairs and hang out talking between takes. "We all just wanted to kick it in each other's living rooms because they were so fabulous," says Alexandra Shipp, who plays an Author Barbie.

Skipper's house is the only one on the block that's purple instead of pink. Leaves are growing out of the roof, and a swing is tied to a protruding branch. Technically, it is Chelsea's tree house—nearly an exact replica, scaled up to fit human actors.

In fact, everything in Barbie Land is built to a specific scale to look "toyetic." "The scale is not lifelike," says Lisa McKnight, the executive vice president at Mattel whose job is specifically to oversee the marketing of Barbie and dolls. For instance, Barbie the character's Corvette is just a little too small for Robbie, just as Barbie the doll's convertible is a little too small for her: The windshield only comes up to her chest.

Gerwig's team didn't just study mid-century furniture trends. The filmmaker also revisited the films of Old Hollywood in order to capture the look of those stories. Rather than using a green screen to

CONTINUED ON PAGE 68

The Dreamhouse slide—a fixture that Robbie personally requested—leads to a painted pool, which the actress could walk across.

Barbie's little pink Corvette was custom-made and was driven by a remote operator.

CONTINUED FROM PAGE 64

ensure that there were only bright blue skies in idyllic Barbie Land, Gerwig's team hand-painted the backdrops to look like old soundstage musicals. In an early scene, Ken tries to interact with a set backdrop, with disastrous results. Many of the props on set were also painted by hand, from the trees to the pool that sits outside Barbie's Dreamhouse and contains no water. "I remember even the bark of the palm trees had different shades of brown, green, and even pink," says McKnight.

Barbie is filled with dance numbers that are heavily influenced by 1940s and 1950s musicals like *Singin' in the Rain*. But Gerwig didn't limit herself to one era. The movie is stuffed with references to all sorts of films, ranging from *Rocky* to *2001: A Space Odyssey* to *Clueless*.

Gerwig obsessed over all the Barbie Land de-

tails, and the props that populate the fantastical space, such as a Barbie version of the book *Moby Dick* on a side table, imbue it with a surprisingly lived-in quality. All the letters in Barbie's mailbox have been scribbled upon in a nonsense language, like a child might write. Barbie devotees know that Pantone 219 C is Barbie's very specific shade of pink; a giant Pantone 219 C chip sits outside the Barbie conference room at Mattel headquarters. But the set used so much pink paint—in that specific color, as well as secondary and tertiary shades—that it exacerbated a worldwide shortage.

The sheer number of pinks in every shot presented their own challenge. "I don't think we have seen or will ever see a film with more pink in it," says producer David Heyman, who helped build another famous fantasy world with the Harry Potter film

series. "And then how to handle that photographically—thank goodness we had [cinematographer] Rodrigo Prieto, who was able to balance all that and create a beautiful and rich palette."

The soundtrack is filled with today's top artists, but even the singers were chosen with intention. Issa Rae, who plays President Barbie, points out that Barbie's image among adults has been buoyed in recent years by Nicki Minaj, who has adopted the name Barbie as one of her personas. Minaj, along with Ice Spice, are the ones remixing Aqua's 1997 "Barbie Girl" song in a wink to Barbie's influence on music throughout the years. "My Barbie association is Nicki Minaj," says Rae. "So it's dope that she is a part of this movie in some way."

Beyond the Barbie immersion course, Gerwig and Baumbach did their own deep dive to dig up even more details about particularly strange or controversial outfits or dolls Mattel produced over the years. Oscar-winning costume designer Jacqueline Durran was charged with replicating some of Barbie's most iconic looks. She had a direct line to Kim Culmone, the head of design for fashion dolls at Mattel, who in turn would search the archives to provide the filmmaking team with references. Every bathing suit and camp shirt was handmade and silk-screened and completely custom.

"Whether it's 1950s ladylike attire or a Western Barbie and Ken look or the roller blades, those looks stick out to me as really toyetic," says Culmone. "And that was important, because even though we were putting Barbie in the real world, there was always a commitment to serve the fans of Barbie with these toyetic references." ❤

Sizing Up *Barbie*

TIME'S FILM CRITIC FOUND
THE MATTEL QUEEN'S
CINEMATIC DEBUT VERY PRETTY
BUT NOT VERY DEEP.

BY STEPHANIE ZACHAREK

THE FALLACY OF BARBIE the doll is that she's supposed to be both the woman you want to be *and* your friend, a molded chunk of plastic—in a brocade evening dress, or a doctor's outfit, or even Jane Goodall's hyper-practical safari suit—that is also supposed to inspire affection. But when you're a child, your future self is not a friend—she's too amorphous for that, and a little too scary. And you may have affection, or any number of conflicted feelings, for your Barbie, but the truth is that she's always living in the moment, her moment, while you're trying to dream your own future into being. Her zigzagging signals aren't a problem—they're the whole point. She's always a little ahead of you, which is why some love her, others hate her, and many, many more fall somewhere into the vast and complex in-between.

With *Barbie* the movie—starring Margot Robbie, also a producer on the film—director Greta Gerwig strives to mine the complexity of Barbie the doll while also keeping everything clever and fun, with a hot-pink exclamation point added where necessary. There are inside jokes, riffs on Gene Kelly–style choreography, and many, many one-line zingers or extended soliloquies about modern womanhood—observations about all that's expected of us, how exhausting it all is, how impossible it is to ever measure up. Gerwig did a great deal of advance press about the movie, assuring us that even though it's about a plastic toy, it's still stuffed with lots of ideas and thought and real feelings. (She and Noah Baumbach co-wrote the script.) For months there had been loads of online chatter about how "subversive" the movie is—how it loves Barbie but also mocks her slightly, and how it makes fun of Mattel executives even though their real-life counterparts are both bankrolling the whole enterprise and hoping to make

Robbie's enthusiastic performance anchors Barbie.

a huge profit off of it. The narrative is that Gerwig has somehow pulled off a coup by taking Mattel's money but using it to create real art, or at least just very smart entertainment.

It's true that *Barbie* does many of the things we've been promised: There is much mocking and loving of Barbie, and plenty of skewering of the suits. But none of those things make it subversive. Instead, it's a movie that's enormously pleased with itself, one that has cut a big slice of perfectly molded plastic cake and eaten it—or pretend-eaten it—too. The things that are good about *Barbie*—Robbie's buoyant, charming performance and Ryan Gosling's go-for-broke turn as perennial boyfriend Ken, as well as the gorgeous, inventive production design—end up being steamrolled by all the things this movie is trying so hard to be. Its playfulness is the arch kind.

Barbie never lets us forget how clever it's being, every exhausting minute.

That's a shame, because the first half hour or so is dazzling and often genuinely funny, a vision that's something close to (though not nearly as weird as) the committed act of imagination Robert Altman pulled off with his marvelous *Popeye*. First, there's a prologue, narrated by Helen Mirren and riffing on Stanley Kubrick's *2001: A Space Odyssey*, explaining the impact of early Barbie on little girls in 1959; she was an exotic and aspirational replacement for their boring old baby dolls, whose job was to train them for motherhood. Gerwig shows these little girls on a rocky beach, dashing their baby dolls to bits after they've seen the curvy miracle that is Barbie. Then Gerwig, production designer Sarah Greenwood, and costume designer Jacqueline Durran launch us right

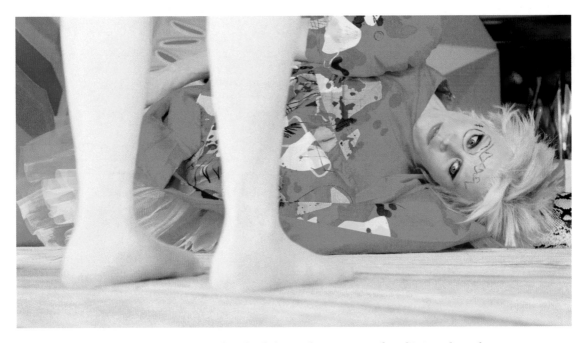

Kate McKinnon's Weird Barbie helps guide Stereotypical Barbie into the real world, where she hopes to solve the mystery of her flat feet—and so much more.

into Barbie Land, with Robbie's approachably glam Barbie walking us through. This is an idyllic community where all the Dreamhouses are open, not only because its denizens have no shame and nothing to hide, but because homes without walls mean they can greet one another each day with the sunrise. "Hi, Barbie!" they call out cheerfully. Everyone in Barbie Land—except the ill-fated pregnant Midge, based on one of Mattel's many discontinued experiments in toy marketing—is named Barbie, and everyone has a meaningful job. There are astronaut Barbies and airline pilot Barbies, as well as an all-Barbie Supreme Court. Garbage collector Barbies, in matching pink jumpsuits, bustle cheerfully along this hamlet's perpetually pristine curbs. This array of Barbies is played by a selection of actors including Hari Nef, Dua Lipa, Alexandra Shipp, and Emma Mackey. The president is also Barbie— she's played by Issa Rae. (In one of the early section's great sight gags, she brushes her long, silky tresses with an overscale oval brush.)

Barbie Land is a world where all the Barbies love and support one another, like a playtime version of the old-fashioned women's college, where the students thrive because there are no men to derail their self-esteem. Robbie's Barbie—she is known,

as a way of differentiating herself from the others, as Stereotypical Barbie, because she is white and has the perfectly sculpted proportions and sunny smile of the Barbie many of us grew up with—is the center of it all. She awakens each morning and throws off her sparkly pink coverlet, her hair a swirl of perfectly curled Saran. She chooses an outfit (with meticulously coordinated accessories) from her enviable wardrobe. Her breakfast is a molded waffle that pops from the toaster unbidden; when she "drinks" from a cup of milk, it's only pretend drinking, because where is that liquid going to go? This becomes a recurring gag in the movie, wearing itself out slowly, but it's delightful at first, particularly because Robbie is so game for all of it. Her eyes sparkle in that vaguely crazed Barbie-like way; her smile has a painted-on quality, but there's warmth there, too. She steps into this role as lightly as if it were a chevron-striped one-piece tailored precisely to her talents.

Barbie also has a boyfriend—one Ken of many Kens. The Kens are played by actors including Kingsley Ben-Adir and Simu Liu. But Gosling's Ken is the best of them, stalwart, in a somewhat neutered way, with his shaggy blond hair, spray-tan bare chest, and vaguely pink lips. The Kens have no real job, other than one known as "Beach," which involves, as you might guess, going to the beach. The Kens are generally not wanted at the Barbies' ubiquitous dance parties—the Barbies generally prefer the company of themselves. And that's why the Kens' existence revolves around the Barbies. As Mirren the narrator tells us, Barbie always has a great day. "But Ken has a great day only if Barbie looks at him." And the moment Robbie does, Gosling's face becomes the visual equivalent of a dream Christmas morning, alight with joy and wonder.

You couldn't, of course, have a whole movie set in this highly artificial world. You need to have a plot, and some tension. And it's when Gerwig airlifts us out of Barbie Land and plunks us down in the real world that the movie's problems begin. Barbie awakens one morning realizing that suddenly, nothing is right. Her hair is messy on the pillow; her waffle is shriveled and burnt. She has begun to have unbidden thoughts about death. Worst of all, her perfectly arched feet have gone flat. (The other Barbies retch in horror at the sight.) For advice, she visits the local wise woman, also known as Weird Barbie (Kate McKinnon), the Barbie who's been "played with too hard," as evidenced by the telltale scribbles on her face. Weird Barbie tells Robbie's confused and forlorn Stereotypical Barbie that her Barbie Land troubles are connected to something that's going on out there in the real world, a point of stress that turns out to involve a Barbie-loving mom, Gloria (America Ferrera), and her preteen daughter, Sasha (Ariana Greenblatt), who are growing apart. Barbie makes the journey to the real world, reluctantly allowing Ken to accompany her. There, he's wowed to learn that men make all the money and basically rule the land. While Barbie becomes more and more involved in the complexity of human problems, Ken educates himself on the wonders of the patriarchy and brings his newfound ideas back to empower the other Kens, who threaten to take over the former utopia known as Barbie Land.

> Robbie is game for it all. Her eyes sparkle in that vaguely crazed Barbie-like way; her smile has a painted-on quality, but there's warmth there, too.

By this point, *Barbie* has begun to do a lot more telling and a lot less showing; its themes are presented like flat lays of Barbie outfits, delivered in lines of dialogue that are supposed to be profound but come off as lifeless. There are still some funny gags—a line about the Kens trying to win over the Barbies by playing their guitars "at" them made me snort. But the good jokes are drowned out by the many self-aware ones, like the way the Mattel executives, all men (the head boob is played by Will Ferrell), sit around a conference table and strategize ways to make more money off selling their idea of "female agency."

The question we're supposed to ask, as our jaws hang open, is "How did the Mattel pooh-bahs let these jokes through?" But those real-life execs, counting their doubloons in advance, know that showing what good sports they are will help rather than hinder them. They're on Team Barbie, after all! And they already have a long list of toy-and-movie tie-ins on the drawing board.

Meanwhile, we're left with *Barbie* the movie, a mosaic of many shiny bits of cleverness with not that much to say. In the pre-release interviews they gave, Gerwig and Robbie insisted their movie is smart about Barbie and what she means to women, even as Mattel executives have said they don't see the film as being particularly feminist. And all parties have insisted that *Barbie* is for everyone. *Barbie* probably is a feminist movie, but only in the most scattershot way.

The movie's capstone is a montage of vintagey-looking home movies (Gerwig culled this footage from the cast and crew), a blur of joyful childhood moments and parents showing warmth and love. By this point, we're supposed to be suitably immersed in the bath of warm, girls-can-do-anything fuzzies the movie is offering us. Those bold, bored little girls we saw at the very beginning of the film, dashing their baby dolls against the rocks, are nowhere in sight. In this Barbie Land, their unruly desires are now just an inconvenience. ♥

The Marketing Machine

THE MOVIE'S UBIQUITOUS
PROMOTION HAD US LIVING IN
A *BARBIE* WORLD.

BY COURTNEY MIFSUD INTREGLIA

Barbie has been everywhere in 2023. To promote the film, Mattel and Warner Bros. engaged in an unprecedented—and ultimately inescapable—marketing blitz that included an array of *Barbie*-focused partnerships and products, including Hot Topic's pink gingham cardigan and Microsoft's hot-pink Xbox custom console and controller faceplates. Mattel also offered a whole line of *Barbie*-inspired dolls, play sets, and accessories, including several of the outfits Margot Robbie wore in the film.

A summer blockbuster typically costs upwards of $100 million to

1. Airbnb redecorated the real-life Barbie Dreamhouse in Malibu, California, in Ken's style for a one-weekend rental opportunity tied to the film's opening.
2. Three-hand date black LiteHide leather watch, Fossil
3. Carry-on roller suitcase, Béis
4. Cold Stone Creamery's "All That Glitters Is Pink" cotton candy ice cream
5. Joybird's Dreamhouse Diane modular chaise sectional
6. Barbie Monopoly board game, Hasbro
7. Burger King restaurants in Brazil offered the BK Barbie Combo, a cheeseburger topped with bacon bits and a bright pink sauce served with a pink vanilla milkshake.
8. Dragon Glassware coffee mugs
9. Impala in-line skates (like the ones Barbie and Ken wear in the movie)
10. Boohoo graphic oversize hoodie
11. Crocs clogs
12. Barbie logo mini backpack, Loungefly
13. Kitsch rhinestone claw clips
14. Fuzzy mini crossbody bag, Hot Topic

market, which meant quite a bit of speculation as to how expensive this campaign must have been. Josh Goldstine, Warner Bros. president of worldwide marketing, declined to comment on the figures directly, instead telling *Variety,* "the reason people think we spent so much is that it's so ubiquitous. That's a combination of paid media and how many partners came to play with us." According to Goldstine, some of the less obvious partnerships, such as Progressive Insurance or Crocs, came by way of licensing deals with Mattel, as well as other brands joining in on the hot-pink zeitgeist

of the movie. "It stopped becoming a marketing campaign and took on the quality of a movement," Goldstine said.

For Mattel—which also owns American Girl, Hot Wheels, and Fisher-Price—the *Barbie* partnership, says CEO Ynon Kreiz, will "serve as a template" for collaborations on other Mattel-owned IP. The company is slated to release a Disney Princess film later this year and another one in early 2024 (Mattel won the license to those toys away from rival Hasbro last year), and a Hot Wheels movie is set for 2025. "We have seen

improving trends, with Barbie's month-to-date POS [point of sale] in July turning positive," Kreiz said in late July, when the toymaker benefitted from the buzz around the film and its July 21 release. Kreiz added that more movie-related toys and products will be released later in the year to meet the continuing strong demand.

For Warner Bros. and Mattel, the hustle has paid off. *Barbie* shattered even the loftiest box office expectations, and many of the partner retailers have sold out of their tie-in products. Barbie showed she can turn pink into green.

"Anywhere else, I'd be a 10,"
Gosling's Ken sings, reeling
from Barbie's ambivalence.
"Is it my destiny to live and
die a life of blond fragility?"

Ken's Complicated Journey

IN MANY WAYS, *BARBIE* IS A
MOVIE ABOUT MALE FRAGILITY.

BY ELIANA DOCKTERMAN

HO KNEW THAT "HE'S just Ken" was more than a marketing joke? The *Barbie* movie centers, of course, on its titular character, played by Margot Robbie. But Ken (Ryan Gosling) plays an important role in the drama as he wrangles with the notion that he's long been an accessory in Barbie's dream life, rather than an equal partner. I'll say the quiet part out loud: Even though this is a movie that leans heavily into a feminine aesthetic and is—as writer-director Greta Gerwig has said—a film at its core for mothers and daughters, Ken has the most intriguing and funniest part to play, offering a searing social commentary on modern man's insecurities, dressed up in bubble-gum pink.

Perhaps we shouldn't have expected less from the mind behind *Lady Bird* and *Little Women.* Gerwig transforms a joke about the forgettable male doll into a meditation on the state of masculinity at

a moment when so many young men, feeling disempowered, have found misguided solace in the patriarchy. It's a B-plot that's so compelling it often outshines the somewhat dated girl-power mantras of *Barbie*'s A-plot.

From the start of the film, Barbie's small rejections sting Ken. He seethes when she talks to other Kens, particularly the one played by Simu Liu, whom he sees as a rival. He doesn't have a real job or home or purpose outside of Barbie. Then Ken leaves Barbie Land, that feminist utopia, and enters the real world, where men run, well, everything. In short, Ken discovers the patriarchy and decides to bring it back to Barbie Land, establishing his own "Kendom."

In a clever bit of screenwriting, Ken cares more about the sartorial manifestations of the patriarchy than the patriarchy itself. He is, after all, a fashion doll. When he discovers that demolishing feminism involves more than donning Sylvester Stallone–inspired fur coats, riding horses, and redecorating Barbie's Dreamhouse into what he dubs

his Mojo Dojo Casa House, he loses interest. He's easily distracted by acting out war games with the other Kens, allowing the Barbies to take Barbie Land back from the boys.

By the end of the movie, Barbie and Ken have to have a serious conversation about their relationship. Barbie makes it clear she's not interested in Ken romantically and urges him to find his own personal passions. The finale not only flips the normal script on female-centric films—in which a woman discovers she doesn't need a man to find her inner power (*Legally Blonde*, *Eat Pray Love*, etc.)—but offers a commentary on how men ought to reassess their own desires outside of their need to both control and depend on women.

Speaking to TIME, producer David Heyman suggested that men of all ages would find resonance with Ken's journey. "I think Ryan is undeniable and so affecting in the film. People really care for Ken, even when he's misguided," Heyman says. "I think a lot of boys and men will find there's a lot to relate to in Ken as they try to find their place in the world. But it's all done with such a light touch and such generosity, and Ryan is just, I think, extraordinary."

Gosling does, indeed, pull off what could have been a tricky character. If Ken weren't so ridiculous, he'd be threatening. Ken isn't an incel, exactly. Short for "involuntary celibate," *incel* is a word that certain men use for themselves to describe a state where they feel rejected by women and resentful

Gosling leads a rebellion of Kens (including Kingsley Ben-Adir and Ncuti Gatwa) against the Barbies.

more of Barbie's attention: He can never stay over because Barbie tells him "every night is girls' night," and while the Barbies live in the Dreamhouses, the Kens don't seem to have their own homes. (Maybe they live on the beach, and that's why Ken's job is, nonsensically, "Beach.")

When Ken enters the real world, people suddenly call him sir and ask for his advice or help. While the men on Venice Beach ogle Barbie, they treat Ken with a certain degree of respect. Ken is enthralled by this newfound power. Unfortunately, he learns that he can't just walk his way into a job as a banker or doctor. He complains to one man in a business suit that his company must not be "doing patriarchy right" if a man without any qualifications can't get a job. The businessman assures him that they *are* doing patriarchy correctly—they just need to hide it better these days than they used to. Eventually Ken decides that if he can't participate in the patriarchy in the real world, he'll bring the philosophy back to Barbie Land, transforming it into the Kendom.

When Ken returns to Barbie Land to preach the gospel of patriarchy, one can't help but think of certain male-rights activists recruiting impressionable young followers. Gerwig isn't the first director to wrestle with this problem in recent years. Watching *Barbie*, I was reminded of last year's Olivia Wilde movie, *Don't Worry Darling*.

These films seemingly have nothing to do with each other; one's a musical romp, the other a sci-fi-inspired psychodrama. But the third-act twist of *Don't Worry Darling*—major spoilers ahead for this fraught film—is that Florence Pugh's character, Alice, isn't actually living in a 1950s suburban utopia. She's trapped in a simulation by her partner, Frank (Harry Styles).

Feeling emasculated by his wife's taxing job as a doctor and his own unemployment, Frank listens to a men's-rights podcast and falls under the influence of its host, played by Chris Pine. Wilde says Pine's character was inspired by Jordan Peterson, whom she describes as a "hero to the incel community." The hypnotic podcast host convinces Frank that both he and Alice would be happier living in a fantasy throwback to an era where the men worked and the women played housewife. Alice eventually figures out the trick and has a violent confrontation with her captor.

Other shows and films have explored similar territory: The excellent 2017 *Black Mirror* episode

toward them as a result. These men spend a lot of time in internet forums bashing feminists and longing for the days when women didn't have jobs, men controlled women's bodies, and men's mere earning power could all but "guarantee" them a sexual partner or wife. These online misogynist groups are a breeding ground for toxic language that has also spilled over into real-world violence.

Ken is more mild-mannered than that. He doesn't have the, um, parts down there to even really understand what sex is. When he tries to kiss Barbie goodnight, she stares at him blankly. When he asks to stay over, she asks innocently what they would do. He charmingly replies that he doesn't know. But the implication is certainly that Ken would prefer

Gosling's Ken (with Robbie, opposite) desperately wants to be the focus of Barbie's life. He becomes particularly jealous when she talks to the Ken played by Simu Liu (above).

"USS Callister" reveals over the course of its runtime that a talented but oft-mocked coder (Jesse Plemons) has stolen the DNA of the people in his life he resents (mostly women of color) and forced them into a simulation where he plays the captain of a *Star Trek*–like spaceship. Emerald Fennell (who makes a cameo in *Barbie*) explored the simmering violence lurking beneath the surface of self-styled "nice guys" in her 2020 thriller, *Promising Young Woman*, even casting actors who cultivated that reputation in other projects, including Adam Brody (*The O.C.*) and Max Greenfield (*New Girl*), to drive home the point.

All of these films draw at least some inspiration from the original book *The Stepford Wives* (and its various film and television adaptations). The satirical feminist horror story chronicles a husband's conspiracy to subjugate his working wife after they move to a community filled with strangely robotic women who live to serve their spouses.

Gosling's portrayal of Ken in *Barbie* is lighter and funnier than these more serious takes on the resentful man who works to repress the women around him. Heyman is right that we empathize with Ken when he's ignored by Barbie and root for him to find his meaning. But at its root, his energy—or "Kenergy"—is not dissimilar from that of the men in these other stories. His feelings of emasculation manifest in shows of aggressive behavior, albeit satirical ones. Like Frank in *Don't Worry Darling*, he seems not just resentful but without purpose in a world where women pursue their passions. Both movies are deeply interested in the idea that modern men feel uncomfortable ceding power to women and what it means for their identity.

What, in the end, are women to do about this male fragility? *Barbie* offers a complicated and not entirely satisfying answer. The Barbies eventually overthrow the Kendom and reach a détente with the Kens: They will give the Kens as much power in Barbie Land as women have in the real world. Just a few judgeships, not half of them. And cabinet positions, but not the presidency. It's not exactly equality, but it's a compromise. Whether such an equilibrium can or should be reached in the real world the film doesn't try to answer. Nor is it necessarily the responsibility of a fun musical romp to do so. In the end, Ken learns that he's "Kenough" without Barbie, a resolution that plays better as a pun than an edict for the modern man. ♥

CHAPTER

3

The Original Influencer

SINCE SHE FIRST ARRIVED, BARBIE HAS
COMMANDED OUR ATTENTION AND
DRIVEN CONVERSATIONS ABOUT FEMINISM,
FASHION, AND SO MUCH MORE.

In 1961, Mattel released a record album, Barbie Sings!, to celebrate her romance with Ken.

How Barbie Helped Raise Generations of Feminists

WHILE SHE'S LONG BEEN ACCUSED OF PERPETUATING SEXIST STEREOTYPES, THE POPULAR DOLL HAS ALSO BEEN A CONDUIT FOR CREATIVITY AND EMPOWERMENT.

BY SARAH SELTZER

ARBIE, THAT MINX, invaded my home against my mother's inclinations, as she did for so many Gen Xers and millennials. Our boomer parents' sensibilities were offended by her frivolous existence. Nonetheless, she wiggled her way in. My family legend has it that our apartment's pioneering Barbie, outfitted in spandex and leg warmers, was a gift from a passive-aggressive friend of the family, the same one who also "accidentally" got my brother and me boxes with lead paint on them.

Regardless of Workin' Out Barbie's origin, she was followed soon thereafter by Astronaut Bar-

bie, wearing pink boots and a shimmery spacesuit, and then a third Barbie, of unknown name, in a flowery dress, less tethered to the modern era and more ready to be absorbed into my pretend games of "olden times" and fairy tales. That was the turning point. Those first few dolls were soon joined by dozens of companions, including Barbie's racially and culturally diverse pals, her little-sister dolls, and one Ken. They arrived on birthdays and Hanukkah, gifts from school friends and relatives, and even occasionally from my parents. My collection became a focal point for playdates at my place. The dolls commandeered the drawer under my bed and spread themselves to all corners of my room during the games my friends and I played with them, practically until we hit puberty.

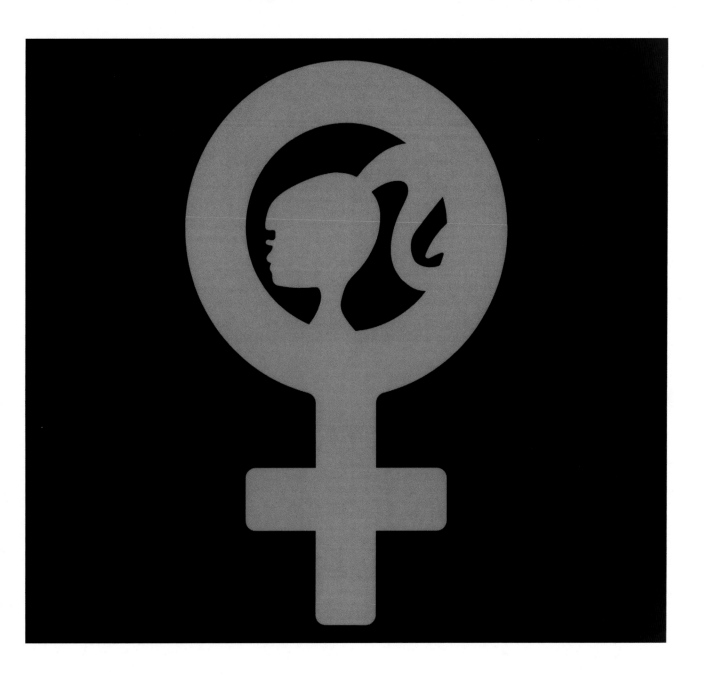

And yet even as I was sliding those ridiculous high heels onto my Barbies' feet, I was also plotting the revolution, to the degree a child can. I was a pint-size feminist, an advocate for reproductive rights, and a self-styled tomboy in homage to my favorite heroines of YA literature. I was not actually a tomboy: I was a bookworm, obsessed with classics of girlhood like *Anne of Green Gables* and *Little Women* and also devouring nonfiction books about mythology, history, and even sports. At the same birthday parties where one friend would bestow me with a lacy pink Barbie outfit, another would buy me a book about "Great American Women" from which I learned to admire very un-Barbielike figures such as Sojourner Truth, the Grimkeé sisters, Rosa Parks, and Eleanor Roosevelt.

That seeming contradiction—Barbie-loving feminist—long puzzled me. I've been mulling over Barbie's impact on my psyche basically since I stopped playing with her, and more recently as Greta Gerwig's live-action *Barbie* movie has put the doll at the center of the discourse. In the pages of a feminist zine that friends started at the end of the '90s, I argued in favor of Barbie, saying that those hours of open-ended imaginary play she fostered helped build me into a creative person and taught me to value independence, storytelling, and collaboration with friends.

As an adult, and a parent, I think the truth is more complicated. I remember unboxing a Barbie and removing her accessories from their plastic slots with a kind of hungry acquisitive need. I remember the crazed, semi-competitive way my best friend and I would demand the very same Barbies from our parents. Now, when I wake up on Saturdays and scroll Instagram, I still trick myself into believing that a great bargain on outfits for the kids, or me, will fill a week's worth of emptiness and exhaustion. Barbie culture helped indoctrinate us into the idea that consuming, accessorizing, having the perfect "stuff" would complete us, thereby lining Mattel's pockets, because we were always left wanting more.

I also remember how horrified I was when, at age 12 or 13, just after I had abandoned Barbie, I discovered that I was no longer growing taller but instead had sprouted hips. Suddenly, jeans and skirts didn't fall straight down on me the way they did on all my Barbies, and I didn't like this development (so to speak) at all. I was being welcomed into a lifetime of typical, but no less painful, body-image angst.

Of course, pernicious messages about consumption and beauty came from many places other than Barbie: TV shows, movies, magazines, older people. But our Barbie dolls, roughly dressed, undressed, and reconfigured, had their role, too. Criticisms of Barbie's negative qualities have predominated discussion of her social impact: those silly heels, the pink car, the completely unrealistic body that would tip over in real life, the whiteness and blondeness, the privileging of fashion and beauty over brains. And yet, so many of us played with her—and we all went to see the movie anyway. We saw it with the gleeful anticipation I used to feel at school when I knew I had a playdate coming up that day and the Barbie drawer would be raided.

Whatever our adulthood looks like today, whether we are gender-nonconforming or ultra-feminine, parents or career-oriented or all of the above, anyone who is not a man has to spend their days negotiating with the ever-present forces of consumerism and monolithic beauty culture that Barbie embodies. Nowadays, we can't just chuck the aspects of society we despise down the laundry chute as we did with our Barbies.

> Barbie provided an easy way for kids, mostly girls, alone and in groups, to control their own narratives, make up their own stories, and indulge in their own fixations.

But maybe we wish we could.

Perhaps that constant negotiation explains why, as generations have (by and large) embraced queerness, feminism, anti-capitalism and, yes, wokeness, they also feel a kind of ownership over this problematic doll franchise. Barbie's plastic-ness, her financial accessibility, her generic quality meant we could turn her into whatever we wanted—including an avatar for our most violent, strange, and wildly imaginative tendencies. Kids tied up their Barbies, dismembered them, acted out conflicts, and even held orgies. Ken was an afterthought, a joke (a fact the film is eager to play with). Whether whole or headless, whether we revered her or destroyed her or both, Barbie was subsumed into our own ideas about how to play. Unlike paper dolls or American Girl dolls that came attached to a historical era or were too expensive to own or play with, Barbie was a *toy* as soon as she came out of the box: We could cut her hair, change her outfit, and immediately make her over in whatever image was on our mind— or forget about her entirely. It was a bit rebellious, taking a doll that was supposed to look a certain way and making her behave *our* way.

Mattel's other '80s franchises, including the She-Ra dolls that I loved before I got into Barbie, didn't have this moldable quality. At my house, Barbie was almost always starring in epic, days-long imaginary games full of love affairs, violence, and betrayals. For others, she was sitting around boardrooms or visiting beauty salons or getting murdered by pirates, or being a murderer herself. Barbie provided an easy way for kids, mostly girls, alone and in groups, to control their own narratives, make up their own stories, and indulge in their own fixations. And in that way, she made the idea of adulthood, and womanhood, something younger girls could try on and experiment with—or they could simply fire her down the hallway like a blonde torpedo. I don't want to get too in the psychological weeds about the cultural ubiquity of girls torturing their woman-shaped

While Barbie comes with a lot of baggage, playing with her (even if it sometimes turns chaotic) can help young girls foster creativity and collaboration.

dolls, or making these comically busty avatars of womanhood hump each other, but it sure is *interesting*, isn't it?

Many wonderful films about girlhood make boys and puberty the focal point or dwell on girls' relationship with their mother. But for so many of us, playing with Barbies was about our relationships with ourselves and our friends and all the ways those experiences blended with the broader culture of materialism and femininity. That's why a smart, feminist director like Greta Gerwig offering her take on Barbie—and doing it in a way that appears to foreground ambivalence, humor, and neon—feels so exciting.

It's not as though we expected Gerwig to offer a full-throated critique of Barbie—the movie, after all, is produced by Mattel. What matters is how the film recognizes Barbie's simple presence in so many of our young lives. It means millions of girls' intense, silly, and personal childhood play is being acknowledged, given the royal Hollywood treatment, and taken both as seriously and unseriously as we took our Barbies themselves. ♥

Sarah Seltzer is the author of the novel The Singer Sisters *(Flatiron, 2024) and an editor at* Lilith Magazine.

The Power of Pink

BARBIECORE—THE STYLE TREND
POPULARIZED BY EVERYONE'S
FAVORITE FASHION DOLL—HAS
TAKEN OVER THE WORLD.

BY CADY LANG

Country singer Kacey Musgraves made a bold statement as she arrived at the 2019 Met Gala in New York City.

BARBIE IS ALWAYS IN style. Look no further than the all-pink outfits filling red carpets, the countless social media posts with rosy themes, and the takeover of pink in street style. The fashion trend, which has been spotted on celebrities including Lizzo and Florence Pugh, as well as on runways such as that of Valentino, who unveiled a collection of hot pink designs in 2022, has been dubbed "Barbiecore" in an homage to the stylish doll, whose brand identity is undeniably feminine and very, very pink.

Barbiecore is soaring thanks to the convergence of multiple cultural moments. The release of the *Barbie* movie comes in a year that finds us well into the resurgence of early-aughts fashion and its bright, sweet styles. According to fashion technology company Lyst's 2022 "Year in Fashion" report, Barbiecore was the top trend of the past year, which peaked in June 2022, when pictures of Margot Rob-

bie as Barbie clad in an all-hot-pink Western outfit were released. The look went viral on TikTok and sparked a 416 percent increase in searches for pink clothing. But the trend has been a mainstay of both celebrity and high fashion for years, cycling in and out of vogue for the past two decades. Darnell-Jamal Lisby, a fashion historian and the assistant curator of fashion at the Cleveland Museum of Art, says Barbiecore has become a staple of fashion in the 21st century, recirculating every few years. "If we hadn't seen it past the early 2000s, I would have just called it a trend," Lisby says. "But it's definitely reiterated every few years in different ways."

Barbie's enduring influence on fashion in the

in anything? And girls could dream up whatever career or type of person they want it to be and try it on for size,'" Stone says. The element of fashion as a way of imagining the future was so important to Handler, Stone says, that Mattel designed Barbie's head to pop off easily to make it easier to change her outfits. "Her mission was to allow girls to have the imaginative kind of play that would allow them to dream about being anything they wanted to be at a time when women couldn't be a lot of things … she wanted them to be able to be astronauts and surgeons, and she was also all about haute couture."

The first Barbie doll sported a high ponytail, a full face of painted-on makeup, and heavy-lidded eyes. She was firmly rooted in a specific idea of femininity, and her clothes reflected that: Barbie came dressed in a form-fitting black-and-white striped strapless swimsuit, accessorized with a pair of black stiletto mules and black cat-eye sunglasses with blue lenses. Additional outfits were unapologetically feminine, miniature versions of clothes that a grown woman would dream of—evening gowns, cocktail dresses, vacation wear, and sundresses. Perhaps it should come as no surprise that one of the first careers Mattel marketed for Barbie was being a fashion model, or that the unrealistic aspects of her appearance, such as her

real world is a direct reflection of Ruth Handler, the woman who created the doll, says Tanya Lee Stone, author of *The Good, The Bad, and the Barbie: A Doll's History and Her Impact on Us*. Handler was a savvy and style-forward businesswoman who created Barbie when she saw that baby dolls and paper dolls dominated the toy market. With Barbie, Handler created a doll that could give little girls the chance to embody their future dreams—whether that was becoming an astronaut, a doctor, or a fashion model. And she had the clothes to match. "The physicality of that kind of play for girls at the time was really limited, so she thought, 'What if I made a three-dimensional model that could look fabulous

perpetually arched feet or her impossible proportions, were made for showcasing fashion.

For Handler, it was important that Barbie represent what a woman could be, and that was reflected in the doll's clothes—an outfit could transport the player to not only a different look but a career or lifestyle. "Unlike play with a baby doll—in which a little girl is pretty much limited to assuming the role of Mommy—Barbie has always represented the fact that a woman has choices," Handler wrote in her memoir, *Dream Doll*. "Even in her early years Barbie did not have to settle for being only Ken's girlfriend or an inveterate shopper. She had the clothes, for example, to launch a career as a nurse, a stewardess, a nightclub singer."

Stone attributes both the current Barbiecore trend and its influence on fashion to one of the foundational elements of the toy's success: marketing. Mattel was one of the first companies to target children in its advertising, as opposed to parents, broadcasting commercials for Barbie dolls during *The Mickey Mouse Club* in the late '50s. This strategy not only led to the toy's immense success but ensured that the doll had a firm and lasting hold on pop culture, as generations of children grew up to be adult consumers. The most telling example of this may be Barbie's ubiquitous association with the color pink. While the original doll, meant as a high-fashion toy, didn't have pink marketing, in the '70s Mattel made a push to market Barbie to young girls instead of adolescent girls, and it used pink as the main color for the doll's brand identity. Now, of course, Barbie is synonymous with the shade, and Pantone has a color called Barbie Pink (219 C), a deep, bright shade of the rosy hue.

Barbie has had her fair share of critiques, especially when it comes to gender and diversity. Although Handler claimed to have created her as a way to empower young girls, the doll has been a lightning rod of controversy, especially in feminist circles, where she's been held up as perpetuating unrealistic body and beauty ideals or promoting singular and outdated gender norms. "She's sometimes a doll we love to hate, but that has staying power, anytime something has controversial elements," Stone points out. "A lot of things were bumpy along the way, but there were also advances that weren't happening elsewhere."

Barbiecore as we know it began with the rise of celebrity fashion figures of the early 2000s, like Paris Hilton, Nicole Richie, and Britney Spears, whose outfits, meticulously covered in tabloids, were hyperfeminine and often pink or glittery, Lisby says. Costuming for films such as *Clueless*, *Legally Blonde*, and *Mean Girls*, featuring distinct female characters in bright pink, also played a role in the trend's popularity. In the late aughts, pop stars became instrumental in helping the trend gain momentum, from Ariana Grande's girly style, which can be traced back to Barbie, to the rapper Nicki Minaj, who has channeled the doll since 2010 through an alter ego known as "the Harajuku Barbie," filling her lyrics, song titles, and album art with references to Barbie and wearing a pink wig and a chain with the Barbie logo. Her fans even call themselves "the Barbz." (Minaj collaborated with Ice Spice on "Barbie World," featuring a remix of "Barbie Girl," for the *Barbie* movie's soundtrack.)

When it comes to the world of high fashion, Pierpaolo Piccioli's 2022 all-pink Valentino fashion show, which spawned its own hot-pink Pantone shade, is obviously top of mind, but the most outsize example of Barbie's influence in fashion may be Jeremy Scott's Spring 2015 collection for Moschino, which firmly centered Barbie and her iconography. At the show, models walked the runway in blonde wigs, pink ruffled evening gowns, and pink sportswear emblazoned with a Moschino logo in the Barbie font, with the model Charlotte Free even racing down the runway in roller skates in a nod to Mattel's Rollerblade Barbie.

Emily Huggard, an assistant professor of fashion communication at Parsons School of Design in New York City, says the trend has taken off because of its playfulness, which is extra appealing in a post-Covid world. She points to other trends that have emerged following the pandemic, like "dopamine dressing," the trend of wearing (often brightly colored) clothes that spark joy or make you feel good, and notes that a common thread is a desire for ease and comfort. "People are really latching on to escapism and things that they know and feel safe with," Huggard says. "When we think about this trend [Barbiecore], it's pretty, it's hot pink, it's not too complex—I think people are craving a time when things felt less heavy."

The lead-up to *Barbie*'s release undoubtedly played a part in the trend's reach, too. Everywhere you look, people have been donning all-pink outfits,

> While Mattel and the Barbie doll have been criticized for promoting narrow beauty ideals, Barbiecore is a trend that everyone can take part in on some level.

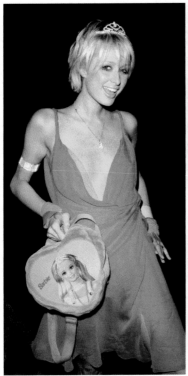

Socialite Paris Hilton (left) sported a Barbie bag and a bright-pink minidress in 2001. Singers Nicki Minaj (center) and Ariana Grande (right) have amplified the popularity of the Barbiecore aesthetic.

with hot pink being especially in demand, a seeming nod to the influence of Robbie's *Barbie* wardrobe. On TikTok, the hashtag #Barbiecore has racked up hundreds of millions of views, while multiple *Barbie* fashion collaborations offering varying degrees of bubblegum and hot-pink clothing and accessories, with brands ranging from Gap to Forever 21, emerged ahead of the movie.

Stone believes that amid political strife and global health scares in recent years, a touch of the fantastical can provide some much-needed respite. "The world is on fire, and all the news is dark," she says. "But there's this bubbly, light, sparkly fantasy phenomenon out there that people can hold onto for a few minutes."

Huggard adds that the appeal of the trend of wearing hot pink lies in its financial accessibility. While Mattel and the Barbie doll have been criticized for promoting narrow beauty ideals, particularly when it comes to size and race, Barbiecore is a trend that everyone can take part in on some level. Hot pink is a bold color that's available at all price points. It's a far more approachable trend to participate in than something like the "quiet luxury" aesthetic, whose expensive minimalism relies on a subtle "if you know, you know" acuity. And that lends itself to virality on TikTok, Huggard

says. Both the trend and the social media platform are tailored to sharing a cultural moment. "We're seeing hot pink at the Met Gala and on runways, and it's being marketed at different levels of the industry and different price points," she says. "It's a wide aesthetic that all people can buy into versus a quiet luxury item. They can invent it in different ways, but they're still wearing it, and it represents something."

Lisby says Barbiecore's current popularity reflects how much society has progressed since the doll was first created, noting that while many might associate Barbie and Barbiecore with hyperfemininity, it can also be a way for people to subvert or play with gender norms. "I see it as a vehicle for taking certain risks in fashion that you haven't really seen in previous generations," he says. "While women may have identified with it more earlier, now men may embrace it as a way of using fashion as a part of their own journey with gender identity or sexual preference."

Ultimately, Barbiecore's allure parallels that of the doll that inspired it—its ability to start a dialogue. "There are so many different conversations you can have because of the Barbie doll," Lisby says. "From corporate marketing to society to our thoughts on gender, race, and size, there's a reason why it's had such incredible staying power." ♥

The Collectors

MEET THE SUPERFANS WHO
CAN'T GET ENOUGH OF BARBIE.

BY EILEEN DASPIN

HEN HE WAS JUST 5 YEARS old, Jian Yang commandeered his first Barbie doll. It was 1984, and the Great Shape Barbie under the family Christmas tree had been intended for Yang's sister. But after he ripped off the wrapping and spied the tiny blonde in her turquoise leotard, Yang knew there was no way he was giving her up. She was too cool of a toy. The preschooler added her to his collection of action figures, where she became the go-to girlfriend to He-Man and Darth Vader, among others.

Today, Yang is 43 and still acquiring Barbies. He owns more than 12,000, which fill several rooms in his home in Singapore. One thing he hates is being described as "the doll guy" in news stories. "You think of some guy who's, like, wearing a pink blazer, or you think of a guy in pink," says Yang, who works as the business director of an ad agency. "I'm that same boy who just keeps buying the toys he likes."

Barbie collectors, like other collectors, come in all ages, genders, nationalities, and levels of obses-sion. Some specialize in vintage Barbies, others in mod Barbies or Signature Barbies issued as limited editions by Mattel. They speak in acronyms unintelligible to ordinary civilians, such as OSS (original swimsuit), TNT (twist 'n' turn waist), and NRFB (never removed from box). There are about 100,000 Barbie collectors around the world, according to Mattel, with Germany's Bettina Dorfmann holding the Guinness World Record for the biggest collection—some 18,500 dolls strong. And the Barbie habit is by no means cheap. Garden-variety collectible Barbies typically range from about $40 to $100, with vintage and designer Barbies sometimes fetching tens of thousands of dollars.

The Barbie-collecting craze began with the first generation that grew up with the doll: baby boomers. As they hit their 40s and started to search for memories of their childhood, Barbie was a natural, a mid-century modern totem. In the interim, millions have grown up with their own emotional attachment to Barbie, generating a self-replenishing supply of new fans. Many collectors consider Barbie an investment, but she can also be a fashion item or a reflection of the collector's personality. "I have so

*Bettina Dorfmann has been collecting
Barbie dolls since she was a child in 1962. She
now owns the world's largest collection.*

many things in common with Barbie," says Azusa Sakamoto, a 41-year-old nail artist and collector in Los Angeles, "like the way Barbie is a happy person. She's very independent. Ken is optional."

The collectible market is at least in part driven by Mattel, which recognized the financial potential early and began issuing special-edition Barbies in the mid-1980s. By the early '90s, the company had launched an adult-collector line that hit $35 million in sales in its first year; by 1995, that figure was approaching $150 million, on total sales of $1 billion. "We're not talking child's play," the *New York Times* wrote. "Collecting Barbie is a serious enterprise for the grown-ups who pursue it, and it is big business for Mattel Inc."

Today, Mattel cultivates collectors and participates in an annual fan convention, though it has no official connection to the group. Instead, the toymaker encourages collecting through limited-edition Barbies; through partnerships with designers, film studios, and celebrities; and through its online catalog of the most desirable models. Mattel's Barbie Signature Membership offers a variety of benefits, including access to limited-edition dolls, website bonus content, and members-only forums and communities.

For Sakamoto, it is the partnerships Mattel has with brands such as PUMA or Moschino that are the most interesting. She has nearly 600 dolls, lives in an apartment decorated in Barbie pink, and even drives a Barbie-themed car. But these days, when Sakamoto buys something Barbie, it tends to be clothing or accessories for herself. She has a closetful of Barbie T-shirts and two pairs of $1,400 Barbie shoes, designed by Charlotte Olympia; her collection includes two Barbie purses, roughly $800 each, from the 2015 Moschino collection. "Moschino isn't really a cheap brand, so I couldn't get them all," Sakamoto says. "If I could buy them all, I would have."

While Mattel works to keep a relationship with collectors, there have been bumps over the years. In 1994, as Beanie Babies took off and began eating into Barbie sales, Mattel produced thousands of Barbies from its collectors' line, which angered some who had paid dearly for the dolls, believing they would be limited editions. A few years later, Mattel refused to allow collector Joe Blitman to include some photos in a Barbie reference book he was writing. Blitman published them anyway, in *Miller's*—a magazine for Barbie collectors—with text complaining of Mattel's "icy corporate fingers." The company responded with a trademark lawsuit against *Miller's*, and collectors all over threatened to boycott Mattel products. It took almost two years for Mattel and *Miller's* publishers to iron out their differences.

Getting down to the nitty-gritty, which Barbies are the best investment? That depends. Some—but not all—new special-edition dolls can appreciate quickly, boosted by speculation. During Paris fashion week in 2014, Mattel released 999 Karl Lagerfeld Barbies priced at $200 each on Net-a-Porter. The edition sold out in less than a day, and many of the dolls just as quickly reappeared on eBay with asking prices from $900 to $3,500. Today there are NRFB Lagerfeld Barbies on eBay for upward of $11,000.

Of course, it's the original Barbie—#1 Ponytail, in collector parlance—who has delivered the biggest bang for the buck. The doll retailed for $3 in 1959, about $32 in 2023 dollars. Today, collector websites cite $25,000 as the going price for an NRFB. The record for a #1 Ponytail was set in May 2006 when a bidder paid $27,450 at a California auction. But such offers don't come around often. If you've got an original Barbie, hang on to her. ♥

—with reporting by Noelle Leblanc

TIME

Editor in Chief Sam Jacobs
Managing Editor Lily Rothman
Creative Director D.W. Pine

Barbie

DOTDASH MEREDITH PREMIUM PUBLISHING
Editorial Director Kostya Kennedy
Creative Director Gary Stewart
Editorial Operations Director Jamie Roth Major
Manager, Editorial Operations Gina Scauzillo
Associate Manager, Editorial Operations Ariel Davis
Editor Rich Sands
Art Director Jennie Chang
Senior Photo Editor C. Tiffany Lee
Writers Shannon Carlin, Eileen Daspin,
Eliana Dockterman, Courtney Misfud Intreglia,
Cady Lang, Sarah Seltzer, Stephanie Zacharek
Copy Chief Tracy Guth Spangler
Researcher Maya Kukes
Production Designer Sandra Jurevics
Premedia Trafficking Supervisor Kayla Story
Associate Director, Premedia Imaging Michael Sturtz
Color Quality Analyst Sarah Schroeder

Vice President & General Manager Jeremy Biloon
Vice President, Group Editorial Director Stephen Orr
Executive Publishing Director Megan Pearlman
Senior Director, Brand Marketing Jean Kennedy
Associate Director, Brand Marketing
Katherine Barnet
Associate Director, Business Development
& Partnerships Nina Reed
Senior Manager, Brand Marketing
Geoffrey Wohlgamuth
Brand Manager, Brand Marketing Mia Rinaldi

Special thanks Gabby Amello, Brad Beatson,
Farah Ameen

DOTDASH MEREDITH
President, Lifestyle Alysia Borsa

Margot Robbie stands tall in Barbie's opening moments.

Credits

Front cover
Barbie™ The Movie Doll Pink
Gingham Dress, Mattel, Inc.

Back cover
(clockwise from top) © 2022
Warner Bros. Entertainment
Inc. All Rights Reserved.;
Courtesy Mattel, Inc.; Gierth/
ullstein/Getty Images

1–3 © 2022 Warner Bros.
Entertainment Inc. All Rights
Reserved.

From Cultural Icon to
Box Office Champ
4, 6, 8 © 2022 Warner Bros.
Entertainment Inc. All Rights
Reserved. **9** (from left) Gareth
Cattermole/Getty Images; Eric
Charbonneau/Shutterstock

America's Sweetheart
11 Courtesy Mattel, Inc.
12–13 Ian Waldie/Getty
Images **15** Chesnot/Getty Im-
ages **16** (right) James Leynse/
Corbis/Getty Images **18, 19**
Ullstein Bild/Granger(2) **20**
Courtesy Mattel, Inc. **21** Frank
May/DPA/Zuma Press **22**

Gierth/ullstein/Getty Images
24, 25 Courtesy Mattel, Inc.
26 Jaap Buitendijk/Courtesy
Warner Bros. **27** Jon Kopaloff/
Getty Images **28–29** Matt
Campbell/AFP/Getty Im-
ages **30** Courtesy Mattel, Inc.
32–39 All photos courtesy
Mattel, Inc. **40–45** All photos
courtesy Mattel, Inc. Shoe icon
created by Ian Rahmadi Kurni-
awan from Noun Project

Bringing Barbie
to Life
46–59 All photos © 2022
Warner Bros. Entertainment
Inc. All Rights Reserved. **60**
(from left) Han Myung-Gu/
Wirelmage/Getty Images;
Courtesy Warner Bros.; Michael
Buckner/Getty Images; Hector
Vivas/Getty Images **61** (from
left) Han Myung-Gu/Wirelm-
age/Getty Images; Chung
Sung-Jun/Getty Images; Stuart
C. Wilson/Getty Images; Samir
Hussein/Wirelmage/Getty
Images **62–69** All photos ©
2022 Warner Bros. Entertain-
ment Inc. All Rights Reserved.
70–73 All photos © 2022
Warner Bros. Entertainment
Inc. All Rights Reserved.

74 (clockwise from top left) ©
2023 Mattel Inc.; Coldstone;
Joybird; Hasbro; Dragon Glass-
ware; Burger King Brasil; Beis;
Fossil **75** (clockwise from top
left) Impala; Crocs; Kitsch; Hot
Topic; Boohoo Hoody; Lounge-
fly **76–81** All photos © 2022
Warner Bros. Entertainment
Inc. All Rights Reserved.

The Original
Influencer
83 Hulton Archive/Getty
Images **85** Illustration by Katie
Kalupson for TIME **87** Richard
Drew/AP **88–89** Raymond
Hall/GC Images/Getty Im-
ages **91** (from left) J. Vespa/
Wirelmage/Getty Images;
Jemal Countess/Getty Images;
Andrew Lipovsky/NBC/Getty
Images **93** Courtesy Azusa
Sakamoto **94** Ina Fassbender/
AFP/Getty Images **95** T ©
2022 Warner Bros. Entertain-
ment Inc. All Rights Reserved.
96 Emily Shur/AUGUST

Heads Up

A FEW YEARS BEFORE HER FILM DEBUT, BARBIE GOT A LONG-OVERDUE MAKEOVER THAT PAVED THE WAY FOR A MORE DIVERSE BARBIE LAND.

In the *Barbie* movie, just about everyone in Barbie Land is named Barbie. That includes characters of a variety of racial backgrounds and body types. The concept of Barbie deviating from the traditional white, blonde, impossibly thin version followed a similar move that Mattel made in 2016. After plummeting sales earlier that decade, the company knew it had to make a change to jump-start the Barbie business. A diverse line of dolls was introduced, including 33 new Barbies in new body types—tall, curvy, and petite—and seven different skin tones. The move paid off: By summer of 2016, profits were back on the rise, and the company has continued to expand the offerings, most recently with a Barbie who has Down syndrome.

Made in the USA
Monee, IL
22 October 2023

45014671R00059

She's Everywhere

Barbie is many things to many people. A movie star, yes, and a doll who's thrived across generations, evolving and changing, inspiring so much thought, some debate, and a whole lot of fun.

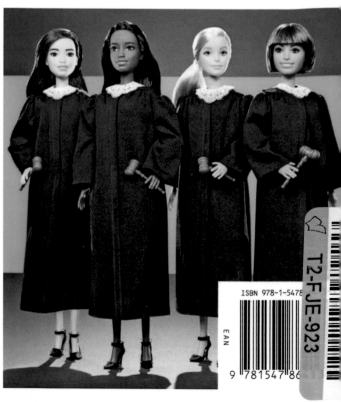